NT PALESTINE

THE LIFE OF JESUS

To my father
who has read the
New Testament every day
for over sixty years

The Life of Jesus

Rachel Billington

Illustrated by Lee Stinson

Hodder
Children's
Books

a division of Hodder Headline plc

First published in Great Britain in 1996
by Hodder Children's Books
a division of Hodder Headline plc
338 Euston Road
London NW1 3BH

A CIP catalogue record for this title is available
from the British Library

ISBN 0 340 67821 6

Typeset by Palimpsest Book Production Limited,
Polmont, Stirlingshire
Printed and bound in Great Britain by
Mackays of Chatham PLC, Chatham, Kent

CONTENTS

Jesus lived nearly two thousand years ago. Most of his life was spent in the land that is now Israel, although parts of Jordan, Syria and Egypt also come into the story. It will be useful to keep looking at the map because Jesus travelled all over the countryside visiting many villages and towns, walking or going by boat.

Until Jesus was about thirty years old, he lived in Nazareth, a village in the hills of Galilee, overlooking a wide and low plain called Jezreel. It was in Galilee, around the Lake of Tiberias, that Jesus did much of his teaching. He was born, however, in Bethlehem, which was in Judaea and not far from the great city of Jerusalem.

The area was mostly inhabited by Jews but there were also Greeks and other races who lived in nearby countries like Samaria and Gadara. Jesus himself was a Jew.

Judaea and Galilee and all the countries round about were part of the Roman Empire, ruled by Caesar Augustus. However, because Rome was such a long way away, they either had their own Jewish kings, who were permitted to rule them as long as they were obedient to Rome, or they had a Roman governor who answered directly to Caesar. When Jesus was grown-up, Galilee was ruled by a Jewish king called Herod Antipas, and Judaea by a Roman governor called Pontius Pilate.

So Jesus spent a lot of his time in a country occupied by foreign soldiers who were on the look-out for any signs of rebellion from the Jews. He also grew up among a people who were longing to be free of Roman rule. The Jewish religion, which centred on the temple at Jerusalem, taught that a saviour or 'Messiah' would come to lead them out of slavery into a kingdom where they would be free.

At that time the religious teachers, the chief priests and the 'Pharisees', who upheld the religion in the community, were very powerful. The rules they followed were based on the Old Testament and were very strict. Their belief in a happy future was based on forecasts by Old Testament prophets. Although these religious men were waiting hopefully for their Messiah, they each wanted to be the one to find him and they took it for granted that he would follow the same rules as they did.

The story you are about to read was written down by four men: Matthew, Mark, Luke and John. John appears in the story himself. He was much loved by Jesus and when Jesus died he entrusted his mother into John's care. Matthew, too, comes into the story. Mark and Luke did not know Jesus personally but, after his death, wrote down what others had told them.

Matthew, Mark, Luke and John often, but not

always, report the same events, sometimes in a different order. I have combined, as best I can, all four tellings, or gospels as they are called, so that they make one continuous history.

CHAPTER ONE

Mary is told by the Angel Gabriel
that she will give birth to Jesus Christ

It was a mild spring evening and a young girl called Mary sat alone in the courtyard of a small house. The house was in a village called Nazareth, set on the top of a high hill. Dreamily, she watched the sun sink below the horizon.

Mary was barely thirteen years old but a few months before, her parents had followed the Jewish custom and arranged her engagement to a man called Joseph who worked as a carpenter. Perhaps that was what she was dreaming about. Or perhaps she was enjoying this quiet end of the day with a thankfulness like a kind of prayer.

Suddenly her peace was broken by a brilliant light, as if the sun had come up again over the hills. Dazzled, she heard a voice call out, 'Hail, Mary, full of grace, the Lord is with you!'

Peering through her fingers, Mary saw the outline of a tall figure dressed in white, arm outstretched. Who was this strange creature? And

1

how did he know her name? Poor Mary was thoroughly scared and bewildered.

'Do not be afraid, Mary,' said the tall figure, who was an angel called Gabriel, 'for God is especially pleased with you.'

Now Mary dared to take her hands from her face and she listened attentively as Gabriel continued, 'Hear me! You will give birth to a son and you will name him Jesus. He will be a great man and will be known as the Son of the Most High. And the Lord will make him king, as his ancestor David was king. And he will reign for ever and ever.'

By now Mary was feeling brave enough to ask a question. 'But how can I have a baby when I'm only engaged and not yet married?'

The Angel Gabriel answered, 'The Holy Spirit will enter you and the power of the Most High will overshadow you. This is why your son will be holy and the Son of God. Listen further! Your elderly cousin Elizabeth is also going to have a baby. Everybody thought she could never become a mother but now she is six months pregnant for, with God's help, anything is possible.'

Mary knelt on the earthy floor and bowed her head in obedience to God's wishes. 'See where I kneel. I am the servant of the Lord. I shall do whatever he asks of me.'

Then the angel and the brilliant light disappeared and the dusky twilight washed back into the courtyard, but Mary stayed outside praying until she felt calmer.

When she finally went in to her family she had made up her mind to visit her cousin as soon as possible. Perhaps Elizabeth would help her understand this extraordinary thing that was going to happen to her.

Elizabeth lived in the hill country of Judaea, a very long journey from Nazareth, so Mary took a donkey to ride on as she crossed the steep, winding paths and rocky uplands.

Early in the morning, when the mists still wreathed the valleys and the sheep and goats had only just been let out to pasture, she said

goodbye to her parents and set off on her journey. The donkey carried baskets filled with bread and olives and goat's cheese and the clothes she would need for her stay.

Mary's cousin Elizabeth was married to a man called Zechariah and they had both longed for a baby all through their marriage but had given up hope. Zechariah was a good and holy man who left his home for part of the year to work as a priest at the temple in Jerusalem. He was offering incense at the altar when an angel appeared beside it.

He was nearly as frightened as Mary had been, but the angel told him, 'Fear not, Zechariah. Your prayers have been heard and your wife, Elizabeth, will bear you a son and you shall name him John. Many people will join you in rejoicing at his birth because he will be great in the eyes of the Lord and he will be filled with the Holy Spirit. He will be a forerunner to the Lord who is to come and he will persuade the wrongdoers back to the path of righteousness.'

Zechariah asked doubtfully, 'How can you expect me to believe this is going to happen? After all, I'm quite old now and so is my wife.'

The angel answered, 'I am Gabriel and I have been sent by God to tell you this good news. Hear me! Because you have not believed me, you will be struck dumb until my prediction comes true.'

And, sure enough, when the angel had vanished and Zechariah staggered from the temple to find the worshippers waiting impatiently outside, he could not speak a single word.

As soon as Zechariah had finished his temple duties, he went home to Elizabeth to find that, much to her delight because she had been ashamed at not being able to bear a child, she had discovered she was pregnant.

Mary arrived at Elizabeth's house, tired but pleased to be there. Her cousin had heard her coming and was standing at the doorway to welcome her.

'Elizabeth!' Mary called out, and the older woman and the young girl kissed warmly.

No one had told Elizabeth that Mary was going to have a baby too but, as she looked at Mary, she was inspired by the Holy Spirit and cried out, 'Blessed are you among women and blessed, too, is your baby!' Which reminded Mary of the angel Gabriel's greeting. Elizabeth continued, 'What have I done to deserve a visit from the mother of my Lord? For when you called my name my baby jumped with joy inside me.'

Now Mary was even more certain that her baby would be the Son of God and, kneeling on the dusty path, she said a prayer of praise and thanksgiving.

Mary stayed with Elizabeth for three months,

helping her prepare for the birth of the baby. Then, soon after Elizabeth had been safely delivered of a boy, Mary found the strength and courage to return home.

Joseph welcomed Mary back but he was surprised when he realised she was pregnant. Naturally, he thought she had been with another man. In those days an engagement was as binding as a marriage and an unfaithful woman was severely punished. However, Joseph was a good man and loved Mary so, instead of making a public example of her, he decided to hide her away until she had the baby. Unhappily, he decided he could no longer make her his wife.

Then one night when he had just fallen asleep after lying awake for a long time worrying, he dreamt that an angel was standing before him.

'Joseph, son of David,' the angel said, 'do not be afraid to marry Mary. Her baby has been given to her by the Holy Spirit. He will be a boy and you must name him Jesus, which means "Saviour". For it is he who will save his people from their sins.'

The next morning this dream was still vivid to Joseph. He decided to obey the angel's commands, so he and Mary were married. In this way a human mother and father were provided for Jesus.

Meanwhile Elizabeth's baby son was now eight

days old and, as was the custom, neighbours and relations came round asking what name the child was to be given. Zechariah was still dumb so Elizabeth told them, 'He shall be called John.'

But a son was usually given his father's name or, at least, a name previously used in the family, so the people didn't believe Elizabeth and gave Zechariah a writing-tablet to make known his choice.

He wrote, 'His name is John.' And at once he could speak again.

As he thanked and praised God, his friends wondered at such a miracle and thought that God must have a very special future planned for this little baby.

CHAPTER TWO

Jesus is born in Bethlehem

The months passed quickly for Mary as she made preparations for her baby's birth. Just before he was due, a ruling went through the land where they lived that every man must go and register his name and his wife's name at the town from where his family first came. This was because the Roman emperor, Caesar Augustus, wanted to find out exactly how many people lived in the faraway corners of his empire. Joseph's family name was David and they had originally come from a small town called Bethlehem. Bethlehem was several days' journey from Nazareth.

So Mary had to leave her comfortable home and mount the donkey again. But this time it was winter and at night it grew dark and cold. In the day it sometimes rained, and when they crossed high ground it snowed, which would have been exhausting even if she hadn't been expecting a baby. Joseph walked beside her leading the donkey, and at night, if they could find nowhere to stay, he wrapped her in his warm sheepskin coat.

After several days, they began to meet other travellers, some going one way, some another, because everyone had to find his family town. At last they saw Bethlehem high up on the hillside in front of them. Smoke from hundreds of fires rose for it was already evening and the air was cold as ice.

By the time they entered the city, it was nearly dark. The narrow streets, the fires from the houses and the lighted windows made the air seemed warmer. But the town was so crowded with people that Joseph knew it would not be easy to find somewhere to stay. He was anxious because Mary had told him that she thought she would have the baby that very night.

He began at once to knock at each door they passed and ask for a room but after hours of walking through the rough streets, with no luck, they found themselves approaching a small inn on the edge of town. It was Joseph's last hope, for beyond it lay only the cold hillside from which they'd come. When the innkeeper saw that Mary was soon to give birth he felt sorry for her. Although he had no room in the inn, he pointed them to a stable where the animals would keep them warm.

To Mary and Joseph the stable was a welcoming place. An ox and ass, large gentle creatures, were eating hay from a manger. Mary began to get everything ready for the birth and, seeing that the manger would make a good crib, she covered the hay with a soft cloth. She laid out a white square with a long strip at one corner in which new babies were always wrapped.

When she had finished her preparations, she waited peacefully.

Later that night, on the dark hills beyond the town, a flickering orange light could be seen. It came from a fire which some shepherds had lit. They camped out every night watching to see that their flocks didn't stray.

Suddenly the whole sky was filled with a dazzling brightness and an angel of the Lord appeared, just like the one who had appeared to Mary and Zechariah. And the shepherds, too, were frightened and hid their faces. The dogs who had been dozing beside them trembled and the sheep huddled together as if a storm were approaching.

But the angel spoke gently. 'Do not be afraid for, behold, I bring you good news of great joy which will come to all the people.'

The shepherds uncovered their eyes.

The angel went on, 'Today a Saviour is born for you in the city of David. And that Saviour is Christ the Lord. You will know this is so because you will find a baby wrapped in swaddling clothes lying in a manger.'

All at once this angel was joined by a whole chorus of angels, singing God's praises:

'Glory to God in the highest,
And Peace to his people on earth!'

They finished their song and suddenly it was dark again. Even the fire had gone out and the shepherds felt cold and stiff as if a long time had passed since they had been lying quietly on the hillside. They stood up, stamped their feet, and an old man said what was in all their minds: 'Let us go to Bethlehem and see this baby.' They put their dogs on guard round the sheep and hurried to the town.

It was nearly dawn when the shepherds reached Bethlehem. The frost made the ground hard underfoot and their breath blew white in the cold air. Only a few early risers, bakers and herdsmen, were stirring from their sleep. The streets were so quiet and empty it hardly seemed the same town as it had been the evening before.

But in one place a lamp glowed as it had all night long and two people who had been awake sat watching by a manger. They were Mary and Joseph and in that manger lay the newborn baby Jesus.

When the shepherds knocked on the door with

their crooks, Joseph rose and let them in. The baby still slept, but as they fell to their knees in worship, he opened his eyes as if he knew who they were and why they had come.

Mary took him on her lap and listened as the shepherds excitedly explained how the angels had burst upon them and instructed them where to find the baby who was to be Saviour of all the world. However hard she tried, it was difficult for Mary to understand that her own little baby was the Messiah for whom the Jewish people had been waiting for hundreds of years. But her heart was filled with love.

The shepherds were so happy that when they left the stable they went through all the town telling anybody they met that they, poor humble shepherds who could neither read nor write, had been chosen to be first to see the Messiah.

In the morning Joseph found a better place for Mary and Jesus to stay so that when their neighbours came round on the eighth day for the naming ceremony, they were no longer sharing a home with animals. Joseph told everybody that the baby was to be called Jesus; everybody knew that the word meant Saviour.

When Jesus was a month old, Joseph and Mary took him to the great temple in Jerusalem. Jerusalem was the centre of the Jewish faith, a big city to country people like Joseph and Mary. They had to come down from the hill on which Bethlehem was perched, pass through a valley and then up to the much steeper hill where Jerusalem had been built. It was a walled city, but outside lay gardens, olive groves and villages.

Joseph and Mary made their way to the temple, the same place where Zechariah had been burning incense when the angel had told him he would have a son. The temple buildings spread over nearly a quarter of the whole city for they were not only used by priests and worshippers but also by teachers and lawyers. The outer courtyards were always crowded and noisy.

Making her way to the altar, Mary presented Jesus to God, which was the tradition with oldest sons, and Joseph handed over the sacrifice of two turtle doves to the priests. They were about to leave when an old man called Simeon saw Jesus. Simeon had been told by God that he would not die until he had seen the Christ child and, much to Joseph and Mary's amazement, he began to cry out praises to God for now, at last, he could die in peace. Then he turned to Mary. 'This child is born to save the people of Israel. But be warned that he will cause you great sorrow.'

Jesus was also recognised by an old widow called Anna, who spent most of her days and nights in prayer. Like Simeon, she thanked God and afterwards went about Jerusalem telling everyone that the Saviour had been born.

Soon afterwards Joseph and Mary took their baby quietly back to Bethlehem. Not many days after they had left, three grand and powerful men, kings in their own countries, arrived in Jerusalem. They were called Caspar, Melchior and Balthasar and they had travelled from the desert regions of the East to find a king whom they said was a far greater king than they were, not only king of the Jews, but of the whole world.

These wise men were also astronomers and could read messages written in the sky by the stars, and at the time of Jesus' birth an unknown star had appeared in their land. They knew it predicted the birth of a king and when it began to move, they had followed it all the way to Jerusalem.

But Jerusalem and the land around was ruled by yet another king, a cruel and wicked man called Herod who had been put in charge by the Romans. He was not at all pleased when he heard that three foreign visitors were looking for a new king on his territory. He didn't want a rival to his throne.

He summoned to his palace all the most important priests and lawyers and other advisers and asked them whether they knew where this baby king could be found. They were very clever and knew all the prophecies so they told him that the child must be in the little town of Bethlehem.

They also knew that he had been born of the family of David.

Herod invited Caspar, Melchior and Balthasar to a magnificent feast in their honour. While they were enjoying themselves, he questioned them closely about where they had first seen the star and finally told them where they would find the child.

'When you have found him,' Herod said, 'and have worshipped him, come back to me with the news so that I, too, can pay him homage.' Of course, he had no intention of paying homage but wanted to know exactly where Jesus was so that he could kill him.

As it turned out, it was easy for the three kings to find their way to Jesus because the star reappeared, more brilliant than ever, and led them directly to the little stone house where Mary and Joseph were living. By now forty days had passed since their baby's birth. Although Mary and Joseph were no longer in a stable, they were poor people and were overawed when the kings, with all their attendants and slaves, crowded into their simple room.

But Caspar, Melchior and Balthasar fell to their knees and bowed their heads in front of the baby. They had each brought a present, which their slaves handed forward. Melchior gave gold, which is the right kind of present for a king; Caspar gave frankincense, which is used to sweeten the air in the presence of God; and Balthasar offered myrrh, which is used in funerals. The wise men knew that this baby's death was to be as important as his life.

Now they were ready to report back what they had seen to wicked King Herod. However, the night before they were to set off back to their own countries, God came to them in a dream and warned them not to see Herod again, so they left by a route which avoided Jerusalem.

Joseph and Mary were also planning to leave Bethlehem, now that Jesus was old enough to travel and the weather was better. They both longed to return to their families in Nazareth and Joseph needed to get back to his carpenter's workshop. But their road would take them near Jerusalem and Joseph also had a warning dream.

An angel spoke to him: 'Arise and take the young child and his mother and flee to Egypt. Stay there until I come to you again and tell you it is safe. For Herod is searching for the baby so that he can kill him.'

Joseph was so frightened that he woke Mary in the middle of the night and they set off on a different road at once. Egypt was about a hundred miles to the south so they had a very long journey ahead.

King Herod was enraged when he discovered the three kings had left his land without reporting back to him. As he didn't know exactly where to find the baby he feared so much, he decided to kill every single little boy who was aged two years or under in Bethlehem and the surrounding towns and villages.

His soldiers went out with their swords and murdered hundreds of innocent babies, tearing them out of their mothers' arms and attacking anyone who tried to stop them. But, of course, it was not only a cruel but also a pointless act, because Jesus was safe in Egypt.

CHAPTER THREE

The childhood of Jesus in Nazareth

Jesus, Mary and Joseph lived in Egypt for two years and then another angel came to Joseph in his sleep.

'Wake up, Joseph,' the angel said. 'Take your little child back to Israel. The man who wanted to kill him is dead.'

This was exciting for the whole family and they had started packing their bags when Joseph heard the frightening news that King Herod's son, Archelaus, had taken his father's place as King of Judaea. Eventually Joseph decided it would be safe enough to return as long as they avoided Jerusalem and went directly to Nazareth.

The family settled comfortably into the life typical of a small town in Galilee. Joseph enjoyed his work as a carpenter, which was a skilled job and made him respected among his neighbours. As Jesus grew up, he was trained as a carpenter, too, so that he could follow in his father's footsteps. He was also taught to read and write by the priests, as all Jewish boys were. Jesus was a handsome boy, big and strong, but also clever and thoughtful for he had been given special gifts by God.

Once a year at the springtime feast of Passover, which marks the escape made by the Jews hundreds of years ago out of the land of Egypt where they had been slaves, Joseph and Mary went to celebrate at the temple in Jerusalem. This was a pilgrimage made by hundreds and thousands of adult Jews so the roads were always crowded with families and the city was filled to overflowing.

As soon as Jesus became twelve years old, he was counted as an adult so he was allowed to make the journey too. The family stayed a week and then started home. Mary left first with the women, who walked more slowly than the men, and Joseph followed later. What neither of them noticed was that Jesus was not with either of them. Mary thought he was with Joseph and Joseph thought he was with Mary, so it was only when they came together on the first night that they realised he had disappeared. They asked all their friends and relations but no one had seen him.

They were very worried because these were dangerous times for a young boy to be lost, alone in a place he didn't know. After all, they could never forget how narrowly he had escaped being killed when he was a baby. As soon as it was light they turned round and travelled the opposite way to everyone else until they were back in Jerusalem again. Even then, they spent three whole days searching the city with no sign of their son.

Then one morning, they came to the temple and saw, to their astonishment, Jesus sitting calmly among the teachers and students. He was involved with the discussions and was obviously impressing everyone with the depth of his knowledge and understanding.

But Mary and Joseph were not impressed. Mary asked reproachfully, 'My son, why have you treated

us like this? Your father and I have been desperately worried. We've been looking for you everywhere.'

'Why did you search?' Jesus answered quietly. 'Surely you knew I would be in my Father's house.'

Mary and Joseph did not understand that he was referring to God, his Father, so they were even more taken aback. But Jesus left the temple and returned to Nazareth with them.

Once more he became Jesus the obedient son of an ordinary carpenter. If Mary looked at him sometimes and wondered what great mysteries the future held, she kept her thoughts to herself.

The Nativity

CHAPTER FOUR

Jesus leaves home and is baptised
by his cousin, John

Meanwhile, Jesus' cousin, John, grew up and left his family to live in wild country where he saw no human being from one day to the next. He dressed in a rough coat made of camel hair with a leather belt round his waist, and he ate locusts, which are insects like large grasshoppers, and honey from the wild bees. Then he began to preach, warning those who visited him, 'Repent of your sins for the kingdom of heaven is at hand.' People began to talk of him as a holy man, a divinely inspired teacher. They said that the ancient prophet Isaiah had forecast his coming as 'a voice crying in the wilderness'.

People flocked to him from Jerusalem, Judaea and the whole Jordan valley and after they had repented of their sins he baptised them in the waters of the river. The excitement grew and word began to go about that this strange and wonderful figure was the longed-for Messiah. But John told them, 'I am baptising you with water but there is one to follow me who is so much more powerful than me that I am not fit to untie his sandal. He will baptise you with the Holy Spirit and with tongues of flame.'

John not only criticised the behaviour of those who came searching for him in the wilderness but also dared to reprove the ruler of the country where he was living, who was called Herod Antipas. He was another son of the wicked King Herod and also ruled Galilee. He had stolen his brother Philip's wife, a woman named Herodias, and married her himself.

It was very brave of John to criticise a ruler who had power of life and death over him and very dangerous.

During this time, Jesus was still living in the remote village of Nazareth. Around him on the slopes of the hills grew olive trees and vineyards, date palms and fig trees. The green grass was grazed by sheep and goats, for Galilee was a fertile country. Below, Jesus could see the wide wheatfields that stretched as far as he could see northwards and as far as the coast of the Mediterranean Sea to the west.

Mary and Joseph had many relations in Nazareth so Jesus had plenty of cousins to play with and grew up in a busy, bustling atmosphere. There he stayed, well out of the public eye, until he was about thirty years old. At that time he left his home and set off to find the place along the river Jordan where his cousin, John, was teaching.

Jesus approached the river among a great crowd of people all waiting to be baptised. After his days of walking down mountain tracks, through lush grasslands and cornfields and into this desolate desert country, he was tired and covered with dust. Nevertheless, John recognised him immediately. 'Why are you coming to me?' he cried. 'I should be the one to be baptised by you.'

But Jesus insisted, 'Let it be this way round for now. This is the way God wants it.'

He went down into the deep, cool river and John poured water over his head. As he was scrambling back up the bank, the clouds opened above his head and a white dove flew down to him as if it were the Spirit of God. To everyone's astonishment, a voice spoke. 'This is my Son in whom I am well pleased.'

At last the time had nearly come for Jesus to start his own work of teaching. First, though, he wanted to be alone so that he could prepare himself with prayer and meditation. He withdrew to a deserted area near a mountain called Jebel Quarantal. It was a forbidding place only inhabited by snakes and wild boar and other dangerous creatures. To purify his mind, Jesus ate nothing for forty days. Eventually, he became hungry and weak. It was then that the Devil saw his chance to tempt Jesus away from his good plans.

He assumed a horribly mocking voice and dared Jesus: 'If you are truly the son of God, then turn this stone into bread.'

'There are more important things in a man's life than bread,' answered Jesus bravely.

Next minute he felt himself transported to the tallest parapet of the temple in Jerusalem and the Devil whispered in his ear: 'If you are the Son of God, throw yourself down, for it is written that angels will hold up the Son of God so that he will not even stub his toe on a pebble.'

But Jesus replied firmly, 'It is also written that you shall not tempt the Lord your God.'

The Devil made one last attempt. This time Jesus found himself on the top of a very high mountain, so high that he could see below him all the kingdoms of the world at the same time.

'If you will worship me,' hissed the Devil, 'all this will be yours.'

But Jesus cried out, 'Get away from me, Satan! It is written in the scriptures that you worship the Lord your God and no one else.'

At these words, the Devil gave up and angels appeared to look after Jesus and make him strong again.

CHAPTER FIVE

Jesus picks his first disciples and
performs his first miracle

When Jesus had recovered, he returned to the banks of the river Jordan and there he met two men, Andrew and John, who had come from Galilee to be baptised by John. When they saw Jesus, they followed him and spent the day with him. They were the first of Jesus' followers or 'disciples'. Later they were joined by Andrew's brother, Simon, whom Jesus renamed Peter because that means 'rock' and his faith was to be the strong foundation for the Christian Church.

Together, the four men made the long journey back to Galilee and stayed at Andrew and Peter's home in a town called Bethsaida where John introduced his brother, James, to Jesus. Bethsaida was a small town on the edge of the stretch of water, as big as a sea, called the Lake of Tiberias. There were many towns and villages all around the lake because it was filled with fish and the men could earn their living by catching them. Peter, James and John were all fishermen.

Soon these three were joined by another disciple called Philip who introduced them to his friend Nathaniel. Nathaniel came from the village of Cana, a few miles down the mountainside from Nazareth.

At first Nathaniel was doubtful that Jesus could be anyone very important. He joked, 'Don't tell me anything good can come out of Nazareth!' The people of Jesus' home town had a reputation for being unsociable and untalented. Once he had met Jesus, however, and heard his teaching, like the others he fell under his spell.

Although Jesus had now left his home in Nazareth for good, he still saw his mother and his family whenever he could.

One day he had brought his disciples to celebrate with him a wedding in Cana, which his mother, Mary, had helped to organise. The feasting had already lasted for a day or two, and so many guests had come that the wine had run out, which was embarrassing for the bride and groom.

Mary, seeing Jesus standing nearby, turned to him and said, 'Look, there is no wine left.' She already knew that her son had special powers and thought that he might do something to help.

Jesus answered, 'That's your affair, Mother, not mine. I am not ready yet to show my power.'

But Mary knew her son well and was not put off. Confidently, she instructed the servants to do whatever Jesus told them.

There were six stone water-pots nearby, usually used for washing, each holding twenty to thirty gallons. Jesus said to the servants, 'Fill the pots with water.' And they filled them to the brim.

'Now pour some out,' he commanded, 'and give a glass to the steward of the feast to taste.'

The steward took a sip without knowing where it had come from; the water had turned into the most delicious wine. Very surprised, he went to compliment the bridegroom. 'Usually, the best wine is served first and the less good is kept until everyone has already had plenty to drink. But you have kept the best wine to the end.'

This was Jesus' first miracle, which he performed out of the kindness of his heart. It made his disciples understand with even more certainty what an extraordinary man they had chosen to follow.

We know Jesus and his disciples travelled, always on foot, round the villages of Galilee and Judaea. Often, and particularly if it was the Sabbath, the Jewish holy day of the week, he would join the priests and Pharisees in their synagogues, and take part in their teaching and discussions. On other days, he talked and taught wherever he might be, indoors or in the open air.

The Jews had always believed that God was a stern and unforgiving master but Jesus taught them that God loved his people and would always forgive them if they were truly sorry when they had done wrong. He also told them that if they loved God and their friends and neighbours they would find everlasting life in heaven.

Sometimes Jesus slept where the day had ended, in a house he had visited or on a mat under the stars. But if it was possible he returned to a town called Capernaum which, like Bethsaida, was on the shores of the Lake of Tiberias. Soon, Capernaum became his principal base.

CHAPTER SIX

Jesus visits Jerusalem and throws out
the money-changers from the temple

When the feast of Passover came round it was natural for Jesus and his disciples to join all the other Jews and journey to Jerusalem, as he had as a child. He was planning to pray quietly and take part in discussions at the temple, as he always did. But when he arrived, he found the outer court-yards filled with noise and confusion. There were cattle-dealers, men selling sheep and others selling doves to be used as sacrifices. Money-changers were seated at their tables changing foreign money into the kind of money that was accepted at the temple.

As soon as Jesus saw what was going on, he was furious and, making a whip of knotted cords, he drove them out, sheep, cattle and all. He swept the coins off the money-changers' tables and then threw over the tables too. He shouted to the men selling the doves, 'Take them out! You must not turn my Father's house into a market-place!'

Naturally, the chief priests were amazed by his high-handed behaviour and asked who had given him authority. Did he have a sign he could show them?

Jesus, who was calmer now, answered, 'Destroy this temple and in three days I will raise it up again.' No one realised that by 'temple' he meant his body. For Jesus already knew how and when he would die. But he also knew that, after three days, he would come back to life.

Jesus stayed in Jerusalem for a week or more, visiting the temple daily. Once, he was passing by a place called Bethesda where there was a pool surrounded by five archways. Here the blind, the lame and the paralysed gathered because many believed that an angel came down to ruffle the waters and that the first person who bathed after this would be cured. One poor old man on a stretcher had lain there waiting for thirty-eight years.

Jesus noticed him and asked, 'Don't you want to be cured?'

The man explained, 'Sir, I have no one to help me into the water so someone else always gets there first.'

'Stand up,' commanded Jesus. 'Now, pick up your stretcher and walk away.'

To his amazement, the man found he was perfectly well and did as Jesus told him.

That night an important Pharisee called Nicodemus came to Jesus privately, wanting to find out more about this strange young man who was a Jew like himself but seemed to go against Jewish teaching. Jesus explained, 'God so loves this world that he has sent his only Son so that whoever believes in him should not die but have eternal life. For God sent the Son into the world not to condemn it but so that he could save it.'

Nicodemus must have been very surprised by this answer but from that time onwards he became a secret follower of Jesus.

When Jesus and his disciples left Jerusalem, they went down to the Jordan valley again, not far from where John was still baptising great crowds. But more and more people turned to Jesus. When this was pointed out to John, he reminded everybody that he had always said he was only the forerunner to one much greater than himself.

Perhaps John had already guessed he would not be free to teach and baptise for much longer. Herod's anger and his wife's had grown stronger as John became more popular. When they were visiting the area where he lived, they had him arrested and thrown into the terrifying stone fortress of Macherus. No one ever escaped from there.

CHAPTER SEVEN

*Jesus meets a Samaritan woman
and cures a nobleman's son*

Jesus was not with John when he was captured or he, too, might have been arrested. When Jesus heard the news, he set off back to Galilee where he had more friends and would be safer. In order to evade capture, he did not follow the usual valley road but went through Samaria, a country to the west.

By the second day, Jesus had already covered nearly fifty miles and, by midday, he was hot, dusty and tired. While the disciples went off to find food at a town called Sychar, Jesus rested near a well under the shade of a palm tree.

After a while a Samaritan woman came to draw water and Jesus asked her, 'May I have a drink?'

The woman was amazed that he had even spoken to her because the Jews despised the Samaritans and the Samaritans hated the Jews. 'How can a Jewish man like you dare ask a favour from a Samaritan woman?' she asked him.

Jesus replied, 'If you only knew who was asking you, you would beg me for living water.'

The woman thought he was talking nonsense. 'You've no bucket and this well is very deep. How do you think you'd get out this living water? Next you'll tell me that you're greater than Jacob, our ancestor who gave us this well.'

'Anyone who drinks water from this well,' continued Jesus, 'will soon be thirsty again, but he who drinks my living water will never be thirsty again.'

'I'd like some of that water,' said the woman, becoming interested. 'It would be nice never to be thirsty again and never to have to come all the way here and draw up the heavy bucket.'

Then Jesus told her to go home and call her husband. But she told him she had no husband. Jesus agreed that she had none now but reminded her that she had lived with five men before. She was amazed that he knew so much about her and decided that he must be a holy prophet. She thought he might help her to work out something that had always worried her: why were the Samaritans taught to worship on the holy mountain while the Jews were taught to worship in the temple at Jerusalem?

Jesus answered, 'It is not important where you worship God; it is the spirit that counts, not the body.'

She was still a bit mystified and said, 'Of course, when the Christ comes he will explain everything.'

Jesus looked straight at her and said, 'I am the Christ.'

They were interrupted by the return of the disciples who, although they were surprised to see Jesus talking to a Samaritan woman, had already learnt not to comment on any of his behaviour that seemed strange to them.

But the Samaritan woman abandoned her water-pot and ran home, telling anyone she met about this man who knew all about her. She felt certain he was the Christ, as he'd said, and her enthusiasm brought many people to see Jesus for themselves. So Jesus stayed in Samaria for two days, teaching and healing the sick and many believed in him.

Eventually he set off again for Galilee, where he was given a warm welcome because many Galileans had heard him speak in Jerusalem during the Passover festival.

He was visiting Cana, the same hillside village where he had turned water into wine, when a nobleman approached him. His son was lying near to death in Capernaum, about twenty miles away. The nobleman begged Jesus to come down and cure him. At first Jesus was reluctant because he was constantly being asked to perform miracles to prove he was the Messiah.

But the desperate father pleaded, 'I beg you, come down before my son dies.'

So Jesus relented. 'Go back home. Your son will live.'

The nobleman believed him and started back. But before he had arrived he was met by servants, racing out to give him the good news. 'Your son is going to recover!' they shouted.

The nobleman asked them at what time his son had begun to improve and they answered, 'The fever went down yesterday at one o'clock in the afternoon.'

The nobleman worked out that this was exactly the time when Jesus had said, 'Your son will

live,' and he and his whole household became his followers.

Jesus' fame was spreading but it was many months since he had returned to his home town of Nazareth. At last, one Sabbath day, he walked up the steep track to his home town and, as usual, went first to teach in the synagogue.

He began by reading a passage from the prophet Isaiah: 'The spirit of God is upon me, because he has chosen me to bring good news to the poor, to give prisoners their freedom and make blind people see.'

When he had finished reading and before he started teaching, everybody was agog to know what this man, the son of Mary and Joseph whom they had known since he had come back from Egypt as a baby, would say next. What miracles would he perform? They were hoping for some grand entertainment. But Jesus knew they didn't really believe he was the Messiah and he was not going to make things easy for them.

'Today,' he said, 'the words you have heard me read have come true.' He meant that he was the one chosen by God. The crowd began to be restive at this but he tested them further by saying, 'I know you want to see miracles such as I performed at Capernaum but I tell you a man is never recognised as a great man in his own country.'

This infuriated his old friends and neighbours.

They leapt up and grabbed hold of Jesus and took him to the edge of the precipice on which the town was built. They planned to hurl him over but Jesus decided to work a kind of miracle after all. Calmly walking through them, he left the town.

CHAPTER EIGHT

Jesus' fame spreads throughout
Galilee and beyond

From now on, Jesus travelled more than ever, always followed by crowds that grew bigger daily. One weekday morning he was teaching by the shores of the Lake of Tiberias. Since they were in the area, Peter, James and John had taken the opportunity to go fishing the night before and their boats were drawn up nearby while they dried their nets. Jesus was so pressed about by people that he could not be seen or heard. So he asked Peter to take him out a little way in his boat. There he could sit comfortably while he talked.

When he had finished speaking, he said to Peter, 'Put out into deep water and let down your nets for a catch.'

'Master,' Peter said, 'we were hard at work all night and caught nothing but, if you say so, I will let down the nets.' To Peter's amazement, when he pulled the nets back in he had caught such a mountain of fish that he had to call over James and John to help him. Even with two boats they could hardly stay afloat, the weight of the fish was so great.

When they had all returned to shore, Peter fell to his knees in front of Jesus, for he was struck again that he was serving an extraordinary man. 'Go, Lord, leave me for I am just an ordinary sinner.'

But Jesus told all the men there, 'Do not be afraid for, from now on, you will be fishers of men.' Jesus knew he needed men like Peter and James and John to help spread his teaching far and wide. Later he chose more men to be his special followers and friends. There were twelve altogether and they are sometimes called the apostles; their names were Peter, Andrew, James, John, Philip, Bartholomew, Thomas, Simon, another James, two called Judas and Matthew.

Matthew, like Peter and Andrew, came from Capernaum, but he was not a poor, uneducated fisherman. He collected tax from the Jews to give to the Roman government, which meant he was very unpopular. He had an office on the main road of the city. Jesus often walked past with his usual group of friends but one day he stopped beside Matthew.

'Follow me,' he said. And Matthew was so pleased to be chosen as one of Jesus' special disciples that he dropped everything and came at once. As a celebration, he gave a party in Jesus' honour.

Lots of townspeople came, including the high and mighty Pharisees and the lawyers. When they saw how many of the despised tax-collectors were there, they complained to the disciples, 'Why do you eat and drink with such odious men?'

Jesus turned and answered for his disciples, 'Healthy people do not need a doctor. I have not come to help good people but to tell sinners to repent of their sins.'

Jesus wanted his message to reach all kinds of people and did not care what the Pharisees thought of him. This made them angry because they believed they were right about everything and had all sorts of rules laid down that they insisted people must follow if they wanted to be good. One of the most important was that you should not work on the Sabbath Day.

But Jesus wanted to show that rules should not be put above other virtues, like kindness, so he often healed people who came to him on the Sabbath. One Sabbath he was preaching in the synagogue when he saw a man with a withered arm in the crowd. He knew that the Pharisees were wondering if he would heal this man so he decided to teach them a lesson.

'Is it lawful,' he asked them, 'to do good or

do harm on the Sabbath Day, to save life or to destroy it?'

No one could think of any answer to this so Jesus turned to the man and said, 'Hold out your hand.' The man lifted up his arm and there was nothing wrong with it any more. The Pharisees were very angry and began to plot to get rid of Jesus.

But Jesus took no notice and continued to travel about teaching and performing miracles. On one occasion when he was back in Capernaum again, resting inside a house, a sick man arrived outside, carried on a mattress by four of his friends. He had a disease called palsy, which meant he trembled all the time. His friends were determined to get him to Jesus but the house was so full of Jesus' admirers that the stretcher couldn't be squeezed through the door. Refusing to give up, the four friends took some tiles off the roof until they had made a hole and then lowered the sick man to the floor at Jesus' feet.

Jesus was impressed by their determination and said to the man, 'Your sins are forgiven.' This made the Pharisees angry again because they thought only God could forgive sins. And they were made even crosser when Jesus told them that, to him, forgiving sins was as easy as curing the sick. He proved his point by telling the man, 'Stand up. Take up your bed and walk.' Which, of course, he did.

The Life of Jesus

When Jesus was near a city called Nain, about twenty-five miles from Capernaum, he did something even more astonishing. He was approaching the town gate with his friends when they met a funeral procession coming out of the walls towards the graveyard. The corpse which was carried among them was that of a young man, the only son of a widow who was weeping bitterly. Jesus felt so sorry for her that he stopped the funeral procession and told the dead man to sit up. To everyone's surprise, he not only sat up but was alive enough to begin speaking immediately.

Jesus spent almost all his time in public, but there were times when he needed to be alone so that he could pray and find more strength to carry on his work. It was so difficult to avoid the crowds that sometimes he spent the night on a boat in the middle of the lake. One evening he climbed up a mountain so high that the stars shone on him through the night like lamps. When he came down the next morning, he had composed a beautiful set of prayers. The crowds who came from Galilee, Judaea and towns even further afield like Tyre and Sidon, listened attentively as he spoke:

'Blessed are the poor, for the kingdom of God will be yours.

'Blessed are the hungry, for you shall be fed.

'Blessed are those who mourn, for you shall be merry.

'Blessed are those who are mocked and insulted by men because of their love for me. You shall be rewarded in heaven.'

And he told them further:

'Love your enemies and do good to those that hate you.

'When a man strikes you on one cheek, offer him the other.

'Do as you would like to be done by.

'Condemn not and you will not be condemned.

'Give and you will be given.'

CHAPTER NINE

*Jesus calms the storm and casts out
devils from a madman*

Jesus' miracles made sure that people listened
to him. Then many came to believe in his
teachings. But the Pharisees continued to be fierce
enemies. Nevertheless, Jesus held discussions with
them and even went to dinner in their houses.

One evening he was sitting at table when a
woman, who was known throughout the town as
a sinner, crouched down beside him and began to
cry so hard that her tears washed over Jesus' dusty
feet until they were quite clean. Unbinding her
long hair, she used it to dry his feet and then,
after kissing them humbly, she rubbed them with
sweet-smelling ointment.

When Jesus' host, a Pharisee called Simon, saw
this, he was quite shocked and thought to himself
that if Jesus were really a holy prophet he would
know that she was a sinful woman and would not
allow her to come close to him.

Jesus guessed what he was thinking and said,

'Simon, there's something I want to say to you.'

'Speak up,' said Simon.

Jesus told him a little story. 'Once upon a time there were two men and one owed two hundred and fifty silver pieces to a debt collector and the other owed fifty pieces. Since neither had any money to repay him, the debt collector let both off.' Jesus looked closely at Simon. 'Which man do you think will love him most?'

'The man who owed him most, I suppose,' said Simon.

'Quite right,' said Jesus. 'Now, this woman here has washed my feet with her tears and dried them with her hair, which you didn't do. She has kissed them and anointed them, which you didn't do.' Again Jesus looked at Simon. 'Indeed she is a great sinner but she has also shown great love and because of that she deserves all my love too.'

And then as Simon said nothing, he turned to the woman. 'Go in peace, your sins are forgiven.'

It was this sort of forgiving generosity that made him so popular with ordinary people. He lived at a time when women took second place to men but he always treated them fairly. Now when he travelled about there were always women in the crowd and some of them became his friends.

The most famous of these was Mary Magdalene (she was called that because she came from a town called Magdala) whom Jesus had cured of a terrible illness. Wherever Jesus travelled, the women would help make arrangements for his and his disciples' sleeping place, their washing and their food. But the women also took part in their discussions.

Sometimes Jesus was so busy that he did not even have time to see his own mother, Mary, and his cousins. Once when they had not seen him for a long time and came searching for him, he said, 'My mother and my family are those who hear the word of God and act upon it.' Mary, who always understood her son better than anyone else, realised that Jesus was not being cold and unloving but that, after living with her in the family for thirty years of his life, now he wanted to spend every minute increasing the family of God.

After one particularly tiring day, he got into a boat on the Lake of Tiberias with some of his disciples. 'Let us cross over to the other side of the lake,' he said.

They set sail and, as they sped quietly along, Jesus settled himself on a cushion at the back of the boat and went to sleep.

They were right in the middle of the vast lake when suddenly the sky darkened, the wind rose and a storm blew up. The waves broke higher and higher over the prow of the boat until water began to pour in and they were in danger of sinking.

Jesus was so exhausted that he slept through

it all, peacefully unaware. The disciples did not want to disturb him but eventually they became terrified and they woke him, shouting above the noise of the storm, 'Master, we are sinking!'

Jesus opened his eyes and looked round disapprovingly at the angry wind and the raging waves. In a moment, the storm went away and all was calm again. Then he turned to the disciples. 'Where is your faith?' he asked them.

Even though the disciples had seen Jesus do many wonderful things, they were frightened to see that he had power over the wind and the waves.

Although the dangerous storm had passed, the wind was still strong and soon the boat had reached the other side of the lake and a country called Gadara.

The moment Jesus stepped ashore, he was confronted by a wild figure who was completely naked. He had originally come from the town but for a long time he had lived rough among the tombs outside the city walls because his mind was filled with devils and he was so mad that he hacked at his own skin with sharp stones. Sometimes people feared he would kill himself so they chained him up like an animal. But he always broke free and escaped to even more remote hiding places.

This unfortunate man fell down at Jesus' feet and began to shriek, 'What do you want with me,

Jesus, son of the Most High? I beg you, do not torture me!'

This was really the devils talking through his mouth because Jesus was already telling them to leave the man alone.

'What is your name?' Jesus asked the devils.

'Legion,' they answered, because there were so many of them. 'Don't cast us into outer darkness,' they pleaded.

Jesus looked around and a herd of pigs, hundreds of them, was grazing nearby. The Jews considered pigs unclean animals so he sent out the devils into the pigs who rushed hysterically around until they fell over the edge of a precipice and were drowned in the lake. Their herdsmen were terrified at the sight and ran to town to tell the story of what had happened.

The men there were furious at losing their valuable animals and drove Jesus out of their country. But the madman was calm and happy. When Jesus climbed back on to the boat, he wanted to come too but Jesus told him to stay behind and spread the news of what God had done for him throughout his country.

The moment Jesus arrived back in Galilee, he was, as always, surrounded by such a crowd of people that he could hardly walk. In the middle of them was a woman who had a bleeding sickness. She had spent all her money on doctors but no one could cure her. She was too timid to approach Jesus directly but she decided that if she could just get near enough to touch him, she would be healed. She crept up behind him and touched the hem of his cloak and sure enough, her bleeding stopped at once.

Jesus turned and cried out, 'Who touched me?'

The woman was too shy to speak and Peter asked Jesus how he could possibly feel one person's touch in such a crowd.

Jesus explained, 'I felt the power go from me.' He knew that he had miraculously cured someone and wanted to know who it was. At length the woman summoned up her courage to confess it had been her and Jesus blessed her.

That very same day, Jesus cured a twelve-year-old girl, the daughter of an important man who ran the synagogue. Like the widow's son at Nain, the girl was already dead when Jesus reached her and he could hear mournful music being played on flutes.

But Jesus told her weeping parents, 'She is only sleeping.' Then he cleared the room of everybody except the parents and Peter, James and John. When the room was peaceful, he breathed new life into her. In a minute she was sitting up, perfectly well again, and Jesus told her rejoicing family to bring her some food. Jesus was always very practical about human needs and he must have thought that being ill, dying and then being brought back to life was sure to make a girl extra hungry.

Although Jesus spent so much time travelling from village to village, town to town, he still could not be everywhere so he realised he needed more help from his disciples. If they separated and went off on their own, between them they could visit many more places. He called them together and told them to go out and heal body and soul in his name: 'Proclaim the message: "The kingdom of Heaven is upon you." Take no gold, silver or copper to fill your purse, no bag for the road, no change of clothes, no stick. Do not fear those who kill the body but cannot kill the soul. Sparrows are worth nothing yet without God's permission none of them can fall to the ground. As for you, even the hairs on your head have been counted. So have no fear.'

Inspired by these words, the disciples went out bravely and taught others what Jesus had taught them.

The Marriage Feast of Cana

CHAPTER TEN

*John the Baptist is murdered but Jesus
teaches forgiveness*

The dangers were growing for Jesus, his twelve
special disciples and even the disciples who
were not so close to him. The chief priests and
Pharisees were angry because they did not believe
that this rebellious young man, who wouldn't
do what they told him, was the Messiah. They
couldn't control him so they hated him. And yet,
however they denied him, his followers grew in
number every day.

But Jesus was also in danger from King Herod
Antipas, who ruled Galilee, and from Pontius
Pilate, the Roman governor of Judaea. A very
important part of their job was to see that there
were no revolts against the Roman government
and Jesus, with his talk of bringing a new kingdom,
sounded to them like the leader of a rebellion.
And there had been many rebellions in the past.
Besides, if he were the Messiah or Saviour, then
they, like all the Jews, assumed he was planning to

'save' his people from their foreign rulers. In fact, anyone who attracted great crowds of supporters frightened them.

Jesus' cousin John the Baptist knew this only too well because he was still locked away in the dark dungeons of Macherus. Herod Antipas would have liked to kill him but didn't dare because so many of the people thought he was a great prophet and he didn't want to risk a revolt against his rule. But Herodias, the wife of Antipas, was more vindictive and was determined to have John dead as soon as possible.

One evening Herod Antipas was celebrating his birthday with a great feast. Herodias had a beautiful daughter by her first marriage who was also famous as a dancer. She was called Salome and was brought into the great dining hall to dance before the King. As she swayed and swirled and spun, the King became so carried away by her performance that he swore to give her anything she wanted from his whole kingdom.

Herodias bent down and whispered in her daughter's ear. Salome listened and then, bowing low to the King, said, 'I would like the head of John the Baptist brought to me here on a tray.' Herod Antipas was not at all pleased by her request but he couldn't break his solemn oath in front of his guests so he ordered soldiers to go to where John was kept chained and cut off his head. The prison was nearby and, while they were still feasting, the head was brought in on a silver tray and presented to Salome.

Salome passed it to her mother and Herodias was triumphant.

Meanwhile John's close friends went to fetch his body, which they buried. Afterwards, they found Jesus and told him about the bloody end to his cousin's life. Jesus and his disciples knew the risks they ran.

Yet Jesus taught about peace and forgiveness. He seldom became angry as he had when he overturned the tables in the temple at Jerusalem. He taught people by example, for they could see

how kind he was and how he healed people and forgave them their sins.

Sometimes, to help them understand what he meant, he told parables or stories. First he would make the crowds sit down on the grass in whatever part of the country they might be. Once he told the parable of a rich man who had two sons. The younger said to his father, 'Father, give me my share of the property,' so the man divided the estate and the younger sold it and went to a faraway country where he wasted all his money having a good time.

Then that country was hit by a severe famine and the only way the son could earn a living was on a farm looking after the pigs. He was so hungry that he would have eaten the pig-swill if he were given the chance, and it struck him that even his father's servants were better paid and fed. He decided to return home and throw himself on his father's mercy.

When he was nearing the house, his father saw him coming and was filled with love for his son. He ran out to meet him, flung his arms round him and kissed him.

The son said, as he had planned, 'Father, I have sinned against God and against you. I am no longer fit to be called your son. Treat me as you would a servant.'

But the father said to his servants, 'Quick, fetch

a tunic, my best one, and put it on him. Put a ring on his finger and shoes on his feet. Kill the fatted calf and let us have a feast to celebrate this wonderful day. For this son of mine that was dead has come back to life, he was lost and now he is found.'

Now the eldest son was out working. On his way home, as he approached the house, he heard music and dancing. He called one of the servants and asked what it meant. The servant told him, 'Your brother has come home and your father has laid on a great feast because he has him back safe and sound.'

The elder son was angry at this and refused to go in so that his father was forced to come out and plead with him. But the elder son was still cross. 'You know how hard I have worked for you all these years, never once disobeying your orders. Yet you have not given me even the smallest party to enjoy with my friends. But now that this other son of yours turns up, having run through all your money with his women, you give a great feast in his honour. Surely that's not fair.'

'My boy,' said the father, 'you are always with me and everything I have is yours. But how could I help celebrating this day? Your brother here was dead and has come back to life, was lost and is found.'

The Life of Jesus

Over and over again Jesus told stories which emphasised that every sinner will be forgiven amid great rejoicing, if only he is truly sorry for what he has done.

CHAPTER ELEVEN

Jesus feeds the five thousand

News of Jesus' growing popularity was constantly being brought to King Herod Antipas who thought to himself anxiously, 'I beheaded John the Baptist but whoever is this other person I keep hearing about?' He would have liked to have seen Jesus for himself but, for the time being, Jesus kept out of his way.

Whenever he could, Jesus tried to escape to a quiet place away from the crowds who followed him everywhere. One day he particularly wanted to talk alone to his disciples because they had been travelling round the country without him. He took a boat with them across the Lake of Tiberias towards Bethsaida and then went further up into the hills beyond.

But even there people found out where he was and came hurrying after him, from towns and villages all around. When Jesus was persuaded to come out to them, he saw a huge multitude stretched out in front of him, all longing to hear him speak. He felt sorry for them and began to teach them and tell them parables. One of them went like this:

'Once upon a time there was a sower who went out to sow his fields with seed. Some of his seed fell on the path where it was trampled on and eaten by birds. Some fell on rocky ground and it grew a little but when the sun rose it withered away because it had no roots. Other seed fell among thistles and when it grew up, the thistles grew too and choked it. But some of the seed fell on good soil and grew strong so that when harvest time came there was a magnificent crop from it.'

The disciples and a few others seated nearest to Jesus admitted to him that they did not quite understand the special meaning of this story and they asked him to explain it.

He told them, 'The sower is sowing the word of God. Those along the path are the men who hear it but then the Devil comes along and carries off the word from their hearts. The seed sown on rocky ground stands for those who receive the word but give up trying to act on it as soon as it stops being easy for them and there are difficulties or dangers. The seed which fell among thistles represents those who hear the word but are overcome by a love of pleasure and money. The seed in good soil represents those who bring a brave and honest heart to their hearing and let their faith grow stronger day by day.'

The disciples felt inspired by this story and hoped they had brave and honest hearts.

The hours passed quickly as Jesus spoke on the hillside and soon afternoon turned to evening and still no one wanted to leave.

The disciples came to Jesus and said, 'Send the people away now so they can find food and somewhere to stay in the villages round about because there is nothing in this barren place for them.'

Jesus looked across at the crowd and then turned back to his disciples. 'Give them food,' he said.

The disciples wondered if he might be joking and Philip said, 'Even if we spend a huge sum – which we haven't got anyway – on buying bread we still wouldn't have enough to give each one a crumb.'

Jesus asked, 'How much bread have we got?'

Andrew answered, 'A boy here has five barley loaves and two fishes. But those won't go far among so many.'

Jesus said, 'Make everybody sit down in groups of fifty.' So they all settled down on the thick grass and the disciples counted up and realised there were five thousand men, women and children.

Then Jesus took the five loaves and, looking up to heaven, he blessed and broke them into

pieces and gave them to his disciples to hand
over to the multitude. Miraculously, there was
enough to go round. When everybody had eaten
as much as they could, Jesus asked the disciples
to collect anything that was left over. In this way
they picked up twelve baskets of crumbs.

CHAPTER TWELVE

Jesus takes Peter, James and John
to a mountain top where they hear the
voice of God

It was no wonder that when such a huge number of people took part in such a miraculous happening, many of them decided that Jesus would make a better king than the one they had. But Jesus didn't want to be king of any country on earth. He sent away the admiring crowds, although they went reluctantly, and then he asked his disciples to set off back across the lake to Bethsaida without him. They got back into the boat and started rowing across the lake. Meanwhile, Jesus climbed up into the hillside and spent the night hours peacefully praying and meditating.

In the early hours of the morning, the boat had reached the middle of the lake, about four or five miles from shore, when the weather became so bad that the white crested waves threatened to overwhelm it. The disciples were rowing hard, like the good strong fishermen they were, but the wind

was against them and they couldn't get themselves out of trouble.

As the first glimmering of dawn silvered the black and raging waves, they saw a pale figure walking towards them on top of the water. They thought it was a ghost and screamed out with terror.

But the strange figure spoke to them. 'Do not be afraid. It is I.' And they recognised the voice of Jesus.

Peter, who was always impetuous, shouted above the roar of the storm, 'Lord, if it is really you, command me to walk over the water towards you!'

'Come,' said Jesus.

Peter was so filled with confidence and love of

Jesus that he jumped out of the boat and walked on top of the waves. But as he got further out and was surrounded by the fierce shriek of the wind, he suddenly lost his nerve and was panic-stricken. At once he felt himself begin to sink. 'Lord, save me!' he shouted, as the water reached his waist.

Jesus stretched out his hand and took hold of him. 'Why do you have so little faith in me?' he asked. 'Why did you doubt I would save you?' The two men stepped into the boat hand in hand and the wind quietened.

Soon after, the disciples were surprised to find that, without any more rowing, they had reached the shore, which was the countryside round Bethsaida. As usual, Jesus was quickly surrounded by people. A blind man was led up to him: Jesus put spittle on his eyelids and laid his hands on the man's head. Then he asked, 'Can you see anything now?'

The man peered round dazedly. 'I think I can see men,' he said, 'but they look more like trees walking.'

Jesus touched his eyes again, and this time the blind man rejoiced that he could see men who looked like men!

They were about sixty miles away from Jerusalem but some Pharisees, who were still trying to prove to the Jews that Jesus was breaking the most important rules of their religion, had travelled all the way from the city to argue with him.

They had already criticised him for healing on the Sabbath Day but now they noticed that Jesus and his disciples did not follow all the complicated rules for washing before a meal. Jesus argued that what made people wicked was killing, stealing and lying, and that rules about things like washing were much less important.

Some of Jesus' followers found his attacks on their religion difficult and their loyalty began to waver. One day Jesus told them, 'I am the bread of life. He that follows me will never be hungry and he that believes my words will never be thirsty. For I have come down from heaven.'

Some of those listening muttered to each other, 'This is Jesus, the carpenter's son. How can he say that he has come down from heaven?' And they turned against him. But still there were thousands more who believed.

By now, the only chance Jesus had to be alone with his disciples was to travel out of Galilee. Once he went to two great cities on the coast of Palestine, called Tyre and Sidon, built on the edge of the deep blue Mediterranean Sea. Soon he was recognised even there and, although among foreigners, he performed a miracle, raising another little girl from her sick-bed.

On another occasion, he took his disciples north

up the river Jordan to a place called Caesarea Philippi. As they struggled over the stony ground, the sun beating down, as hot as an oven, he asked them, 'Who do men say I am?'

Peter answered that some thought he was John the Baptist come back to life and others that he was some sort of a prophet. 'But, as for me,' Peter said, 'I know that you are Christ, the son of the living God.'

Jesus was pleased by Peter's faith, but he chose that moment to tell all the disciples that some time, not too far away, he would have to go back to Jerusalem where he would face his death. He reminded them that the most important thing was the way they lived their lives and that they must never be afraid of dying.

Three of Jesus' disciples were especially close to him: Peter, and the brothers James and John – particularly John. Perhaps after telling them that he would die soon and that they, too, must risk death if they were to continue as his followers, Jesus wanted to give them a wonderful experience.

Six days later he made these three follow him as he climbed up a steep mountain, called Mount Hermon. With the sun blazing overhead, they climbed higher and higher until the green grass had turned to dark rock and nothing grew and nothing lived, except a few lizards who darted away into secret crevices as they approached.

When they finally reached the mountain top, the sky, glittering with the afternoon sun, filled all the space around them. Exhausted, the disciples collapsed on the ground for a rest. But Jesus went a little distance from them and began to pray.

The three men were just about asleep when, through half-closed eyes, they saw that Jesus had begun to shine. His face and skin shimmered as the sun shimmered overhead, and his clothes sent out sparks of light. He did not look like a human being any more and they realised he was talking to the prophets Elijah and Moses, who had died over a thousand years before.

A moment later, a dense cloud descended to the

mountain top and a voice, coming from the middle of it, echoed in their ears. 'This is my Son in whom I am well pleased. Listen to his message.'

Peter, James and John were filled with terror and awe as they realised they had heard the Word of God and they flung themselves on their faces. But Jesus came over and lifted them up, saying, 'Rise, and have no fear.' When they opened their eyes, they saw only the face of their master, no longer gleaming with supernatural light but looking at them kindly.

CHAPTER THIRTEEN

Jesus travels to Jerusalem and stays
nearby with Martha and Mary

From now on Jesus was preparing himself and his disciples for when he would go to Jerusalem and his life would end. He wanted to leave more than twelve men to spread his message after he had died so he appointed seventy-two more to travel on his behalf, going ahead of him to cities and villages. He warned them that he was sending them out 'like lambs to the wolves'. But they reported back to him that they were often received with great friendliness.

In the autumn a great holy day came due when nearly as many people travelled to Jerusalem as for Passover. It was called the Feast of Tabernacles and was a kind of harvest festival when the Jews gave thanks to God for all the good things that grow in the world. At first Jesus said he would not go to Jerusalem because it was too dangerous, so some of the disciples went ahead. Then he changed his mind and followed them.

On his way he passed once again through the unfriendly country of Samaria. As he entered one village, ten lepers who were outcasts because of their disease, which made their flesh rot right back to the bone, heard of his arrival. They stood some way off from him and shouted as loudly as their illness allowed them, 'Jesus! Master! Have pity on us!'

When he saw them, he commanded, as if he had already cured them, 'Go at once and show yourselves to your priests.'

They went off and while they were on their way, they found the leprosy had left them and their skin was healed. One of them, a Samaritan, while the other nine were Jews, finding himself cured, turned back, praising God at the top of his voice. He reached Jesus and, full of gratitude, knelt in front of him.

Jesus said to his followers, 'Surely all ten were healed. Where are the other nine? Why is it that this one alone has come back to praise God and he a foreigner?' Then Jesus turned to the Samaritan. 'Get up now and go on your way. Your faith has saved you.'

Since he never carried money or food, Jesus relied on friends or friends of friends to give him meals and somewhere to sleep. After all, he had told his disciples, 'Life is more than food, the body more than clothes.' One of the houses where he stayed most often belonged to two sisters called Martha and Mary, who lived with their younger brother, Lazarus. The house was in a little village called Bethany, about two miles east of Jerusalem.

Martha was a very good housekeeper and always welcomed Jesus with water to wash in, clean linen, well-cooked food and a comfortable bed. She made sure Jesus was short of nothing.

One evening, he came into the house, as usual surrounded by friends and followers, and while he rested he began to talk to them.

Mary soon seated herself on the ground at his feet and listened attentively. Martha, however, had so much to do that she had no time to sit down and scurried about doing things that seemed quite essential to her, like filling up the oil-lamps, removing the dirty plates and making sure her guests' goblets were filled.

She became hotter and hotter and crosser and crosser that her sister was sitting peacefully hearing what Jesus had to say while she drove herself to exhaustion. Suddenly she could contain her irritation no longer and burst out to Jesus, 'Lord, don't you find it odd that Mary is leaving me to do all the work? Tell her to get up and give me some help.'

Jesus took Martha's hand and drew her to him kindly. 'Martha, Martha, you are in such a state over so many little things that you have overlooked the one really important thing: my presence here with you now. Mary is quite right to sit and listen to me while I'm here with you, and I will not tell her to give that up.'

It was not that Jesus was ungrateful to Martha for her hard work but that he wanted to point out that sometimes it is even more important to sit quietly and listen to the voice of God.

It was around this time that Jesus taught his disciples the prayer that so many people know by heart. It came about quite simply. Jesus was praying on his own when one of his disciples came up to him and said, 'Lord, teach us how to pray, as John the Baptist taught his followers.'

Jesus answered, 'Say this: "Our Father, who art in heaven, hallowed be Thy name; Thy kingdom come, Thy will be done on earth as it is in heaven. Give us this day our daily bread and forgive us our trespasses as we forgive those who trespass against us. Lead us not into temptation but deliver us from evil."'

Afterwards he told them that their Father in heaven would give them whatever they wanted if they only took the trouble to ask. Perhaps he made them laugh when he ended by saying, 'Is there a father among you who will offer his son a snake when he asks for a fish? Or a scorpion when he asks for an egg? If you, then, bad as you are, know how to give your children what is good for them, how much more will the heavenly Father give the Holy Spirit to those who ask for him?'

CHAPTER FOURTEEN

Jesus raises Lazarus from the dead

When Jesus eventually arrived at Jerusalem, the festival was already part of the way through and he immediately went to the temple where he began to teach. As always, his sophisticated city audience were amazed that a poor carpenter's son seemed so clever and well educated. They were also surprised that he dared speak so openly when everybody knew that the chief priests and the Pharisees were his mortal enemies. Some Jews even began to wonder if their priests had decided that, after all, Jesus was the Saviour they were all hoping for.

But the chief priests were only waiting for the right moment and soon they lost patience and sent some temple guards to arrest Jesus. The guards hung around for a little while, listening to Jesus speak, and became so impressed that they didn't arrest him.

The chief priests and Pharisees were furious when the guards came back without him but they were unrepentant. 'We've never heard anyone say such wonderful things in such a wonderful way as this man,' they explained.

'You're just as easily led astray as the uneducated idiots who follow him round,' retorted the Pharisees disgustedly. But they still hadn't stopped Jesus teaching.

Nevertheless Jesus made some other people angry who did not want to believe what he told them and, on the last day of the festival, a crowd of men began to throw stones at him. Jesus escaped them by hiding in the temple, which was like a maze with many courtyards and buildings. Then, when night fell, he escaped from the city.

After this experience Jesus thought it wise to leave the area round Jerusalem once more and he travelled far up the river Jordan until he reached the wilderness where his cousin John had baptised people before Herod Antipas had beheaded him.

Jesus stayed there for much of the winter. People came from miles around to see him because by now nearly everybody had heard of Jesus of Nazareth. They watched him teach and perform miracles and said to each other, 'All we have heard about this man is true.' They admired him even more than they had John the Baptist and many believed he was the Saviour they had been waiting for.

Jesus was still in this remote region when he

received a message from Martha and Mary, telling him that Lazarus had fallen sick. Obviously they hoped and expected that Jesus would do for a friend what he had done for so many others and come and cure Lazarus.

When Jesus heard the news he reacted strangely, saying, 'This illness will not end in death but will bring glory to the Son of God,' which, of course, meant himself. But, even though he was fond of Lazarus, he did not set out at once. Two days had passed before he said to his disciples, 'Let us go back to Judaea.'

The disciples knew the risks involved in going so close to Jerusalem. 'Master,' they warned him, 'it's hardly any time since the Jews tried to stone you in Jerusalem. How can you be planning to go back into the area?'

They set out together anyway, on the difficult and dangerous journey. But it seemed they were too late, for by the time they arrived Lazarus was not only dead but had been put into his tomb four days earlier. In fact, many of his friends had come the short distance from Jerusalem to mourn his death.

As soon as the sisters heard that Jesus was nearing the house, Martha rushed out to meet him. 'If you had been here, Lord,' she called out reproachfully, 'my brother would not have died.'

Jesus said, 'Your brother will rise again.'

'I know he will rise again on the Day of Judgement,' Martha agreed sadly.

'I am the resurrection and the life,' Jesus responded. 'If a man has faith in me, even if he dies, he shall come to life again. Do you believe this is true?'

'Lord, I do believe it,' replied Martha. 'I am sure that you are the Messiah, the Son of God come down to earth.'

Then Martha went to find Mary and, taking her to one side, told her, 'The Master is here and would like to see you.'

Mary hurried off to find Jesus, who was still waiting where he had spoken to Martha. When the mourners saw Mary leave the house, some of them followed after her because they assumed she was going to pray at Lazarus' tomb.

As soon as Mary caught sight of Jesus, she knelt down at his feet and cried out, just as her sister had, 'Oh, Lord, if only you had been here my brother would not have died!'

When Jesus saw her weeping and her companions weeping, he sighed deeply and was very moved. 'Where have you laid him?' he asked.

They replied, 'Come and see.' Jesus then began to weep, too, and the mourners exclaimed, 'He must have loved him very much!'

One or two added quietly, 'Why couldn't he

have saved Lazarus from death? After all, he could make the blind see.'

Jesus sighed even more deeply and walked over to the tomb. It was a cave cut out of rocks and the opening was sealed by a huge boulder. 'Roll away the boulder,' Jesus ordered.

Martha, who was always practical, was surprised by this and warned Jesus, 'Remember, he has been dead for four days and his body will have begun to decay.'

But Jesus spoke firmly. 'Haven't I told you that if you believe strongly enough you will see the wonders of God?'

So they rolled away the boulder and Jesus looked to heaven and said, 'Father, thank you for listening to me. I know you always answer my prayers, but I am speaking for the sake of the people standing round me so that they believe that it was you who sent me here.'

Then he raised his voice in a great cry: 'Lazarus, come out!'

At this command, and much to everyone's amazement, the dead man shuffled slowly out, his hands and feet still wound in linen bands and a cloth over his face.

'Unbind him,' said Jesus. 'Let him free.' As soon as they had unbound him, Lazarus stood alive and well before them, just as if he had never died at all.

Many of those who had come to visit Mary and had seen Jesus perform the miracle were trustworthy and believed in him. But some went to the Pharisees and reported what he had done.

The chief priests and Pharisees immediately arranged a special meeting to discuss the situation. 'What action are we taking?' asked one Pharisee angrily. 'This man is performing all kinds of miracles. If we leave him alone much longer, the whole populace will believe in him.'

'Then the Romans will think he's leading a Jewish rebellion and come and sweep away our temple and our nation too,' agreed another, just as crossly.

A third, called Caiaphas, who was high priest that year, shouted, 'You're all fools! Use your heads. It's obvious that we must make sure that this man dies. For what is the death of one man to the fate of a whole nation?'

They began to plot and plan exactly how they would bring about the death of Jesus.

Once again, Jesus left Judaea and this time he went to a town called Ephraim, which was on a rocky hillside bordering the desert. It was not as far from Jerusalem as Samaria or Galilee but it was far enough for Jesus to be safe during his last few months of freedom.

CHAPTER FIFTEEN

*Jesus welcomes the little children
on his last journey*

As spring approached and wild flowers decorated the green hillsides, the time came round again for the festival of Passover. It was three years since Jesus had left his life as a carpenter in Nazareth and become a teacher, travelling from one place to another. Now he knew that it was only a few weeks before he would die.

Leaving the safety of Ephraim he set off south with his followers. As they walked along, he took his twelve apostles away from the others and told them exactly what would happen to him. 'We are now going to Jerusalem and all that was written by the ancient prophets will come true. I will be handed over to a foreign power; I will be mocked, abused and spat upon. Then I will be whipped and killed. But on the third day I will rise again.'

But the apostles still thought he would be declared king of their country, in the same way Herod had been king and Herod Antipas was now, and they could not understand what he was talking about.

So they continued on this, the last long journey they would take with Jesus. Among the crowd were a great many children, whose parents wanted Jesus to bless them. When the disciples saw them pushing forward girls and boys hardly more than babies, they tried to send them away, but Jesus asked for the children to be led right up to him. 'Let the little children come to me. Do not try to stop them, for the kingdom of God belongs to such as these. I tell you that unless you become like a little child you will not be able to enter the kingdom of God.'

After a couple of days' walking, they reached the great city of Jericho, a green oasis of date palms and vineyards after miles of yellow desert. As usual, the sick were waiting for Jesus and he had already healed two blind beggars even before he had entered the city walls. He was walking through the narrow streets, with their sandy-coloured houses as yellow as the desert outside, when he was spotted by a man called Zacheus.

Zacheus was a man who made sure the Jews paid their taxes to the Romans so he was not popular. He was very rich but also very small and could not see Jesus over the top of the crowds that surrounded him. Then he had the

Jesus blesses the children

bright idea of climbing up a sycamore tree nearby.

As Jesus passed under this tree, he looked up and said, 'Zacheus, come down quickly. I need to stay in your house today.'

Zacheus climbed down as fast as a monkey and eagerly welcomed Jesus into his home. But those around muttered disapprovingly, 'He has gone in to be the guest of a sinner,' they said.

Zacheus could guess what they were saying and he stood face to face with Jesus and said, 'I promise you right now, Lord, that I will give half my money to charity and, if anyone thinks I have cheated him, I will pay him back four times as much as I owed.'

Jesus was pleased at such a change in a man who had previously cared only about money. Yet again he had proved that even the worst sort of person could change and become good.

Meanwhile, in Jerusalem, everybody was wondering when and if Jesus would dare show his face. Jews had already gathered from all over the country and they asked each other, 'What do you think? Perhaps he's not going to come, after all.'

Many knew that the chief priests and Pharisees had given orders that anyone who saw Jesus should report to them so that they could have him arrested.

Despite all this, six days before Passover Jesus

arrived in Bethany. He went, as usual, to stay with Martha and Mary and Lazarus, who was, now, perfectly well.

It was evening, and Jesus and his disciples were tired, hot and dusty from their long walk. They might have liked an evening of peace and quiet before entering Jerusalem the next morning. But Jesus was so famous now that many people wanted to meet him and the sisters decided to give a dinner in his honour. Martha, the practical one, served the food, Lazarus sat beside him and all the disciples were round about. There was even a leper, called Simon, whom Jesus had cured of his disease. There was also a disciple called Judas Iscariot, whom none of the other disciples quite trusted. They suspected that he took any money they had to share between them, and spent it on himself.

While Martha worked, Mary was preparing a surprise for Jesus. She had used up all their money on a pound of sweet-smelling oil, which only the rich could afford to buy because it came all the way from India, but she wanted to show that she knew Jesus was a king, even if he did not live in a palace like Herod Antipas or Pontius Pilate, who was the Roman governor of Judaea. She thought that Jesus was a high priest too, even if he often preached on a mountainside instead of in a temple.

Mary approached Jesus, cradling the marble jar

of precious oil. As the room fell silent, she broke the seal and poured the oil over Jesus, anointing his head and feet, as if he was a king. The small room was filled with a wonderful perfume. As Mary worked, she began to cry because she was so sad at the dangers Jesus must face in the next few days. Her tears fell on Jesus' feet so she kissed them humbly and wiped them dry with her long black hair.

Before anyone else could comment on her behaviour, Judas burst out rudely, 'Why wasn't this perfume sold for the fortune it cost and the money given to the poor?' He wasn't saying this because he really cared about the poor but to try to cover his tracks, so that no one suspected he was a thief.

But Jesus turned on him fiercely. 'Leave Mary alone,' he said. 'Why do you want to upset her? It is a good thing she has done for me. You will always have the poor among you and you can help them whenever you like, but you will not always have me. She has done her very best for me. She has anointed me for my burial ahead of time.'

Then he turned from Judas to everybody else in the room. 'I tell you this: whenever and wherever my story is told, what Mary has done tonight will be remembered and she will be honoured for it.'

CHAPTER SIXTEEN

*Palm Sunday: Jesus enters Jerusalem
in triumph*

The next morning, very early, Jesus told his
disciples they had a job to do for him. He sent
them to a nearby village called Bephage and told
them that they would see a young donkey tied up
which no one had yet ridden. 'Untether it,' he told
them, 'and bring it to me here. If anyone questions
you, say, "Our Master has need of it."'

The two went on their errand and found the
donkey tied to a door in the street. While they
were untying him, the owner appeared and asked
what they were doing.

They answered, 'Our Master needs it,' and the
owner allowed them to lead it back to Jesus.

As Jesus made his preparations for entering into
Jerusalem, more and more people gathered, not
only his followers but others curious to see the
man who had brought back to life someone who
had been dead and buried for four whole days.

The Pharisees even debated whether they

shouldn't kill Lazarus so people would no longer believe that he had miraculously come back from the dead. They were still planning to kill Jesus but because he was so well known they had to find a real reason to do so, or, at least, a reason that could be made to look like a real reason.

If the Jews believed a man had committed a crime punishable by death, then, by law, they had to take him to their Roman governor. The high priest would need to convince Pontius Pilate that Jesus deserved to die. The Pharisees kept hoping that Jesus would break the Roman law as well as their own religious observances.

Perhaps the Pharisees expected Jesus to creep quietly into Jerusalem and try to avoid them but Jesus always did the opposite of what was expected. He rode up the steep hill to the city as if he were a king entering his kingdom. Certainly his little donkey was not very royal, although his disciples had thrown a cloak over her bony back, but the crowds were not put off by that.

They may have known the prophecy from the Old Testament that the king would enter humbly, riding a young donkey. But even if they didn't, they recognised that Jesus was king of the poor, and they didn't expect him to ride in a chariot like their Roman rulers.

Jesus always made it clear that he was one of the people, even if he was also the Messiah and a worker of miracles, and they ran beside him, cheering and shouting. Some became so carried away with excitement that they threw their cloaks before the donkey's hoofs so that Jesus would not be covered in dust from the road. Others, who had no cloaks, tore down palm leaves from the trees lining the road and laid them down before him like an unrolling carpet.

'Hosanna!' the crowds shouted over and over again. 'Blessed is he who comes in the name of the Lord! Hosanna in the highest!'

Jesus was still more famous in Galilee than in Jerusalem so there were those who asked, 'Who is he?' And others called back, 'Jesus of Nazareth!'

Some Pharisees in the crowd were angry at this hero's welcome and told Jesus to tell his followers to keep quiet. But Jesus answered, 'Let me tell you, if my followers were silent the very stones in the road would shout aloud instead.' He was not going to have them spoil such a day of triumph.

Once Jesus was inside the city, he went straight to the temple and was angry to see that the buying and selling of money and sacrificial doves was going on just as it had been three years before. He drove the traders outside, crying, 'This should be a house of prayer, but you have turned it into a den of thieves.'

Once they had gone, he began to teach and the lawyers and chief priests were desperate to seize him but they didn't dare go near when he was surrounded by so many supporters. Instead, they sent in some spies, who pretended to be interested in what he had to say but really wanted to catch him breaking the law so that they could hand him over to Pontius Pilate.

One of them, pretending to be friendly, put a question to him. 'Master, we know that you are full of good sense. You bow to no one, but teach, in all honesty, proper behaviour. So tell us, may we or may we not pay taxes to the Roman emperor?'

They knew that the men who followed Jesus hated having to give money to the Romans and thought that Jesus would please them by saying they should no longer pay. But Jesus saw through their trick easily and said, 'Show me a silver coin.' They brought one. 'Now,' he continued, 'whose head is pictured here and whose name?'

'Caesar's,' they replied.

'Very well,' he said. 'Then pay to Caesar what is due to Caesar and to God what is due to God.'

The spies had failed to prove that Jesus wanted to overthrow the Roman rule and he was able to continue his teaching.

A little later, he looked up and noticed how the rich dropped their large offerings into the temple collecting box, and then he saw a poor widow come along and put in two small copper coins. Jesus had always maintained that you didn't have to be rich to be received into the kingdom of God, and now he said, 'I tell you this, this poor widow has given more than anyone. Those others had more money than they needed but she, who didn't have enough for herself, has given everything she has.'

All day long the chief priests were hoping to catch out Jesus with some remark for which he could be arrested. When evening came they had failed. However, if Jesus had stayed on in Jerusalem, they might have tried to kill him under the cover of dark when he was no longer surrounded by such big crowds. Just before nightfall he left the city and walked out to Bethany where he stayed with Martha and Mary.

The next morning and for several mornings after, Jesus walked early into Jerusalem, took part in discussions in the temple during the day, and returned to the safety of Bethany at night.

CHAPTER SEVENTEEN

Jesus is betrayed by Judas

It was now Wednesday, two days before Passover, and Jesus spent some of the time at Bethany and some of the time quietly with his disciples in a garden on the outskirts of Jerusalem, called Gethsemane, which was in an olive grove on the Mount of Olives. The disciples needed reassurance, because they were beginning to realise that Jesus really would die. They wanted to know when his kingdom would come.

He told them, 'No one knows the exact hour and day, not even the angels in heaven, not even myself, only God, the Father.' Jesus taught his disciples that they must be prepared and awake always, for the kingdom of God could come at any time. He also told them how they would suffer when he was gone but also how they would eventually find great and glorious happiness.

When night fell, they returned once more to Bethany where they knew Martha would look after them with her usual efficiency. But one of the twelve disciples slipped away on his own and went to Jerusalem. It was Judas, hiding his face so that he wouldn't be recognised, sliding silently through the dark streets, with their archways and steep alleys.

It took him about an hour to get to the temple buildings and there he pulled the sleeve of one of the guards and asked to be taken to the chief priests. The guard asked who he was, and was surprised when he heard the name of one of Jesus' disciples. He hurried him into the temple through a side entrance.

The chief priests had waited a long time for someone to betray Jesus and they were delighted that it should be one of his closest friends.

'How much will you pay me,' Judas asked, 'if I tell you when and where will be the best place to capture Jesus?'

The chief priests offered him thirty pieces of silver, which was a great deal of money although very little for the life of the Son of God.

Judas left the temple as secretly as he'd had come to it and, from then on, he was looking for a time and a place where the chief priests could arrest Jesus without being seen by the crowds. The best chance, he decided, would be when it was dark and when Jesus had only a few people with him.

CHAPTER EIGHTEEN

The last supper, and Jesus is arrested

The next day, Thursday, was the day before Passover and Jesus had new instructions for Peter and John. This time, he wanted them to find a room where they could all have a last supper together.

'As soon as you set foot in the city,' he told them, 'a man will meet you carrying a water-jar.' This would be an unusual sight because women usually collected water from the well. Jesus continued, 'Follow him into a house and give this message to the owner: "The Master asks, where is the guest room where I may eat the Passover meal with my disciples?" He will show you a large room upstairs, with table and chairs all ready. Make the preparations there.'

Peter and John went off obediently and everything turned out just as Jesus had said. They went out again and bought the lamb, which it was the custom to eat at Passover, and the bread and wine.

That evening Jesus took his place at the table with his disciples seated round him, John and Peter on either side. 'How happy I am to eat this Passover supper with you before my death!' he exclaimed, glad to be surrounded by his closest companions, but they began to argue about who was greatest among them so Jesus decided to teach them a lesson in humility. He rose from the table, took off his cloak and, bending low, began to wash the disciples' feet. This made Peter very uncomfortable and he cried, 'I will never let you wash my feet!'

But Jesus insisted, telling them that a master must never think himself more important than his servants. Then he put on his cloak again and came back to the table, saying, 'Now I have set you an example which you all must follow.' But as the supper continued he became distressed and eventually cried, 'It is a dreadful truth that one of you is going to betray me!'

His disciples were shocked and could hardly believe what he had said. One after the other, they asked, 'Do you mean me, Lord?' And then Peter signalled to John, who was leaning close to Jesus, to ask who it was.

And Jesus answered, 'It is the man to whom I give this piece of bread after I have dipped it into the soup dish.'

Judas was face to face with him and Jesus gave

it to him. 'Do you mean me, Master?' Judas whispered.

Jesus nodded and said to him quietly, so that no one else heard, 'Do what you have to do, quickly.' At once Judas left the room but the other disciples still did not understand, assuming that Jesus had sent him to buy something for the festival or to give money to the poor.

The celebration continued without him. Jesus took up a loaf of bread, blessed it, broke it into pieces, and gave it to his disciples, saying, 'This is my body which I have broken for you. Take it and eat it in my memory.' Then he held up a cup of wine and said, 'This is my blood which will be shed so that your sins may be forgiven. Drink it in memory of me.'

They talked far into the night and Jesus prepared them for when he would be gone. He said, 'You must love one another as I have loved you.'

Then Peter asked, 'Where are you going?'

Jesus answered, 'I'm going somewhere you cannot follow.'

'I'll follow you anywhere,' Peter insisted, 'to prison or to death. I would die for you!' And all the disciples cried out that they would die for their master.

But Jesus shook his head. 'Believe me, Peter, before tonight is over and the morning cock has crowed twice, you will deny three times that you know me.'

Peter refused to believe it but Jesus told them how they would all run away. He said, 'You will have many sufferings in this world but, take heart, I will be with you.'

It was late at night when they finished supper and, before leaving the safety of that upstairs room, they gave themselves courage by singing a hymn of praise to God.

Then Jesus went again to the garden of Gethsemane. Telling the rest of his disciples to wait for him, he went further under the shadowy trees with Peter and James and John. He became more and more unhappy, because the time had nearly come when he must die. He told them, 'My heart is ready to break with grief. Stay here and keep awake until I come back.'

So he went alone even deeper into the darkness and, crouching low on the ground, prayed to God: 'Father, you can do anything. If it is possible, take this cup of suffering from me. But not because it is what I want, but because it is what you want.'

Out of the night sky, an angel appeared, bringing Jesus light and strength. Even so, Jesus was in great agony because he was bearing the pain of the sins of all the world. As he prayed, he began to sweat and the drops fell darkly to the ground like drops of blood. Eventually he went back to find his three friends but they were so tired and unhappy that they had fallen fast asleep.

'Oh, Peter!' Jesus woke his friend reproachfully. 'Couldn't you watch with me for even one hour?' But he understood what they were feeling for he added, 'I know you mean to stay awake but your bodies are just not strong enough.'

Three times Jesus went to pray and three times he came back to find the disciples asleep. The third time, he said sadly, 'What, still resting?' And then he raised his voice. 'Get up now. The time has come. I am betrayed into the hands of sinners. My betrayer is approaching at this very moment. Let us go out and meet him.'

Through the twisted trunks of the olive trees they saw Judas coming, accompanied by a great band of priests and Pharisees, temple guards and Roman soldiers. The light from the lanterns they carried lit up their clubs and made the silver blades of their swords gleam brightly.

Judas said to the soldiers, 'Grab hold of the man whom I kiss.' And he went up to Jesus and kissed him, saying, 'Hail, Master!'

Jesus looked at him steadily. 'Friend, why are you here? To betray me with a kiss?' Then he turned to the priests. 'Who are you looking for?'

They answered, 'Jesus of Nazareth.'

'I am he.' Jesus stepped closer. 'Arrest me but leave my followers alone.'

When Peter saw what was happening, he drew his sword and cut off the right ear of the high priest's servant, who was called Malchus. But Jesus told Peter, 'Put your sword back into its sheath. He who lives by the sword will die by the sword.' And he touched the servant's ear so that it was healed again. 'Do you not know that if I prayed to God, my Father, twelve legions of angels would come to rescue me?'

Then he turned to his captors. 'Why have you brought swords and sticks as if I were a common thief? You have seen me teaching in the temple day after day but you did not touch me. Now it is night and you have the power of darkness and evil.'

The Life of Jesus

As the soldiers and guards prepared to lead him off, the disciples, frightened that they, too, would be arrested, ran away. So Jesus was taken all by himself, hands bound, to be questioned by the high priest.

CHAPTER NINETEEN

Jesus is questioned and beaten

First of all Jesus was brought in front of Annas, a previous high priest, who asked him about his teaching and his disciples. Jesus answered that he had spoken openly before the world and suggested Annas ask his questions of those who had heard him speak. One of the officers thought he was being rude and struck him across the face. Jesus said quietly, 'If I have spoken wrongly, then prove it. If I have spoken rightly, then why strike me?'

Some of the other soldiers blindfolded him and beat him more, shouting mockingly, 'Go on, give us a prophecy! Tell us who is hitting you!'

Soon Annas realised he was getting nowhere and passed Jesus through the hallways and galleries of the palace to Caiaphas, his son-in-law and the high priest, whom he hoped would have more luck in making Jesus say something that the Romans would agree was punishable by death.

John, who had friends inside the palace, had returned to follow Jesus quite soon after his arrest.

Now Peter gathered his courage together and, with John's help, managed to get into the courtyard of the palace. It was a cold night so a big fire had been lit and, as Peter was warming himself, a maidservant caught sight of his face.

'You're one of the men who went round with Jesus of Nazareth!' she said, accusingly. 'You're a disciple, aren't you?'

'Whatever are you talking about!' replied Peter. 'Of course I don't know him!' And he hurried off to the gateway just as the cock crowed. But the maid followed him out and said to some people standing around, 'Look, here's one of the disciples of that man Jesus who's just been arrested. You can tell he comes from Galilee by his accent.'

Peter turned away and swore angrily for the second time that he had had nothing to do with Jesus. But the bystanders had heard the maidservant and had heard Peter speak, too, and they wouldn't leave him alone. Among them was a relation of Malchus, whose ear Peter had cut off, and this man approached him confidently.

'Of course you're one of them! I recognise you from the garden.'

Then Peter panicked and began cursing and swearing that he was nothing whatsoever to do with Jesus. For the third time, he yelled, 'Do you hear? I don't know the man!'

Just as he said these words the cock crowed for

the second time and then Peter remembered what Jesus had told him: that before the cock crowed twice he would deny him three times. He rushed outside and wept bitterly.

Meanwhile, inside the palace, Jesus was being questioned by Caiaphas and the chief priests. They wanted to send him to Pontius Pilate, who had the power to execute him. They found witnesses who told all kinds of lies about what Jesus had said and done. But Jesus would not answer any of their questions.

At length they said to him, 'Tell us, are you the Messiah, the Son of God?'

And Jesus spoke. 'That is true. I am. I will tell you, further, that you will see the Son of Man sitting at the right hand of God, trailing clouds of glory.'

At this the priests tore their clothes and screamed, 'Now he has blasphemed. We don't need witnesses any more! He deserves to die!' They spat in Jesus' face and beat him and, in the first grey light of morning, they had him led to Pontius Pilate.

As well as Peter and John, a third disciple had been hanging round Caiaphas' palace all night long, waiting to see if Jesus was condemned. This was Judas. When he saw Jesus being led out, he suddenly understood the terrible thing he had done by betraying his master, and was overcome with remorse. He forced his way into the presence of the chief priests and tried to give the thirty pieces of silver back to them. 'I have sinned!' he cried. 'I have condemned an innocent man to death!'

But the priests didn't want to hear any of this. As far as they were concerned, he had served his purpose and that was the end of it. 'What do we care?' they replied. 'That's your problem.'

In despair, Judas flung down the money on to the stone floor of the temple and ran out. But where could he go? His terrible sin made the whole world seem black and hopeless. Wretched and alone, he walked out to a field and hanged himself from a tree.

CHAPTER TWENTY

Jesus is condemned to die

Pontius Pilate questioned Jesus in the pillared
hall of judgement inside the great palace that
wicked King Herod had built. Pilate sat on a raised
platform and Jesus stood before him, hands tied,
face and body already bruised and bleeding. He
had not slept all night and now the new day would
bring him new suffering.

'Are you the King of the Jews?' Pilate asked,
because if Jesus admitted this, then he would
be guilty of trying to overthrow the Roman
government.

'That is true,' Jesus answered. 'But my kingdom
is not of this world.' And he said more, which made
Pilate see that he was holding an innocent man.
When he realised that Jesus came from Galilee, he
thought he could avoid responsibility by sending
him over to Herod Antipas, who ruled that part
of the country and was staying in Jerusalem for
Passover. Herod Antipas was keen to see the man
about whom he had heard so much, and hoped he

might see a miracle for himself. But Jesus refused to answer any of his questions and in the end Herod Antipas gave up, as Annas had earlier, and sent him back to Pilate.

As Pilate was questioning Jesus further, a message was brought from his wife: 'Have nothing to do with this innocent man. Last night I had a terrifying nightmare about him.' But the chief priests insisted to Pilate that there was every reason to condemn Jesus to death because he had started a rebellion, which had spread from Galilee all the way to Judaea.

It was the custom at Passover to release one convicted prisoner, and Pilate had in his gaol a notorious murderer and rebel called Barabbas. A crowd had gathered outside, now that it was morning, and Pilate went out to them. 'Which man would you like me to release?' he asked. 'Barabbas? Or Jesus, called the Messiah?'

Now the chief priests had persuaded the rabble – not Jesus' followers, of course, but people from Jerusalem who didn't know him – to ask for the release of Barabbas and the death of Jesus, so they cried, 'Barabbas! Barabbas!'

'Then what shall I do with Jesus of Nazareth?' asked Pilate. 'He has done no wrong.'

But the rabble didn't care about that and screamed even louder, 'Crucify him! Crucify him!'

Still Pilate hesitated, and said, 'I will punish

him and then let him go, for he is not guilty.' So he handed Jesus over to the Roman soldiers. They had no interest in who he was or wasn't. They tore his clothes off his back and beat him with long-thonged whips. Afterwards they amused themselves by placing a purple cloak round his shoulders and a crown made of thorny branches on his head. 'Hail, King of the Jews!' they shouted mockingly.

Once again Pilate had Jesus paraded before the rabble, and again said that he was innocent and should be released. But the rabble cried even more furiously, 'Crucify him! Crucify him!'

'Shall I crucify your king?' shouted Pilate.

But the cry came back, 'We have no king but Caesar!'

So then Pontius Pilate gave in and, calling for a bowl of water, he washed his hands in it, saying, 'See, I am not to blame for the death of this innocent man.'

But the rabble yelled, 'We'll bear the blame! His blood will be on us and on our children!'

So the soldiers laid the heavy wooden cross over Jesus' bleeding back and told him he must carry it up the steep road to the hill where he would be crucified.

CHAPTER TWENTY-ONE

Jesus is crucified

Jesus was already very weak from his beating and soon he fell under the weight of the cross. The soldiers didn't want him to die before he could be crucified so they forced a man called Simon, up from the country for the festival, to help him carry the cross. As Jesus stumbled slowly up the winding street, he was followed by a procession of men, women and children, the women weeping and wailing. Among them were his mother Mary, and Mary Magdalene whom he had cured. Somewhere in the crowd, too, as near Jesus as he could get, was his favourite disciple, John.

At length Jesus arrived at the hill called Calvary or, in Hebrew, Golgotha, meaning the place of the skull. First the soldiers nailed Jesus' wrists and feet to the cross and then it was set in a hole in the ground and hoisted upright. Despite his agony, Jesus felt sorry for the soldiers who were commanded to do such a cruel thing, and he said, 'Father, forgive them for they do not understand what they are doing.' But the soldiers couldn't have cared less; they entertained themselves by rolling dice to see who would get Jesus' cloak.

Pilate had ordered that a sign should be nailed above Jesus' head. On it was written in Hebrew, Greek and Latin, 'Jesus of Nazareth, King of the Jews'. When the chief priests saw it they were angry and complained that it should have read, 'This is Jesus who said he was King of the Jews'. But Pilate refused to change it.

Jesus was not being crucified on his own. Two thieves were nailed to crosses on either side of him. Despite their own pain, they were watching everything that happened to Jesus, the crowds of his followers, the rabble who mocked him and the priests who were enjoying his humiliation. When Jesus' cross was hoisted up between the thieves, one of them shouted out scornfully, 'If you really are the Saviour, why don't you save yourself – and us too, while you're about it?'

But the other thief told him off. 'Have you no fear of God when you're on your way to death? Besides, we deserved our sentences, unlike this man who has done nothing wrong.' Then he turned his head towards Jesus. 'Remember me, Jesus, when you come into your kingdom.'

Jesus answered, 'Truly I say to you, this day you will be with me in Paradise.'

At the foot of the cross stood the women who

had faithfully followed Jesus all the way to this terrible place of death. John was also still with them. Jesus looked down pityingly on his mother, who would so soon lose her son, and called for John, whom he loved so much, to stand beside her. Then he said, 'Mother, behold your son. Son, behold your mother.' He knew that John would take her into his home and look after her.

At midday the bright sky was overwhelmed by a darkness like night, and for three hours the sun gave no light.

At three o'clock, Jesus called out, 'My God, my God, why have you forsaken me?' Some people thought he was crying for help, but then he said, 'I am thirsty,' and a soldier poked up to him a spear with a sponge dipped in sour vinegar on the end. He drank and immediately afterwards cried out in a loud voice, loud enough for all to hear, 'My work is done!'

Just before he died, he whispered the prayer that every Jewish child repeated before sleep, 'Father, into your hands I commend my spirit.'

Now Jesus' work really was completed: he had died on the cross to save all the people of the world from their sins. His head fell on to his chest. And, as his life came to an end, great earthquakes made the ground rock and split apart. Tombs cracked open and the curtain in front of the holiest part of the temple, where Jesus had taught, was torn from top to bottom.

When the Roman soldiers on guard saw these strange happenings, they were frightened and their captain said, 'There's no doubt this was the Son of God.'

After a while, slowly and fearfully, the crowds drifted back down the hill. Only the most faithful of Jesus' followers continued to watch and pray.

In the late afternoon, a rich man called Joseph, a secret follower of Jesus from the Jewish town of Arimathaea, went to Pilate and asked permission to take Jesus' body down from the cross and bury it.

Jesus appears to Mary Magdalene at the tomb

He and Jesus' followers wanted to do this quickly because the next day was their Sabbath and a day of rest. Pilate sent a soldier to make certain Jesus was dead. The soldier would have broken his legs as he did to the two thieves but when he found Jesus already dead he pierced his side with his spear and blood and water flowed from the wound.

Joseph lowered the cross, took the nails out of Jesus' wrists and feet and then wound his body in a white linen cloth. He had Jesus carried to a garden where he owned a tomb newly carved out of the rock. Mary and the other women met Joseph there and watched as Jesus was laid inside this tomb. They wanted to anoint him, as was the custom, with spices and herbs but could not do it till the day after the Sabbath, so they left him alone.

But the chief priests and Pharisees were worried because Jesus had said, 'In three days I will rise again.' They went to Pilate and asked him to put a guard on the tomb in case Jesus' friends stole his body and pretended he had risen from the dead. Pilate agreed and a huge boulder was rolled across the mouth of the cave and soldiers were placed on guard.

Jesus' body lay in that dark place, wound in the white sheets of death, for that night and the following day and night. Outside, in the peaceful, leafy garden, the guards kept watch.

CHAPTER TWENTY-TWO

Jesus rises from the dead

The garden was silent. It was two or three in the morning, and there was not a breath of wind; the birds still slept and so did the guards. Suddenly they were woken by a noise like thunder, and saw, through half-open eyes, that the boulder covering the entrance to the tomb had been rolled aside and on it, in a blaze of brightness, was an angel.

Terrified, the guards fled back to the city and told the priests what they had seen. The priests were terrified too, but only in case word got about that Jesus had disappeared from his grave in mysterious circumstances. They promised the guards a good sum of money if they told no one what they had seen but instead put it about that Jesus' disciples had stolen his body.

Very early on in the same morning, so early that the sun had not yet risen and the air was cold as winter, Mary Magdalene went with some other women followers of Jesus to the tomb. Knowing nothing of what had happened earlier on that Sunday, they were carrying spices with which to anoint Jesus' body. As they walked they wondered how they would roll back the heavy boulder to get inside the cave.

But when they arrived, they found, to their astonishment, that there were no guards and that the tomb gaped open. Nervously, step by step, they ventured into the dank darkness.

Suddenly, just like the guards before them, they were surrounded by a brilliant light and an angel appeared, clothed in a long white garment. 'You have nothing to fear,' he said, as they shrank away in terror. 'I know that you are looking for Jesus of Nazareth who was crucified. But why are you looking for the living among the dead? He is not here. He has come back to life as he said he would. Behold where he was laid!'

The women looked and saw the empty tomb and the white burial sheets in which Jesus' body had been wrapped.

The angel continued, 'Remember what he told you when he was still in Galilee: "The Son of Man must be given into the hands of sinful men and be crucified and on the third day rise out of the tomb."' And the women remembered that Jesus had spoken these words to them.

'Go quickly now,' said the angel, 'and tell the disciples that Jesus has risen from the dead.' As suddenly as the angel had appeared he was gone, taking the brightness with him.

Mary Magdalene and the other women were filled with excitement and rushed out of the tomb, out of the garden and into the city to find where the disciples were hiding for fear of being arrested. They did not tell anyone the news on the way, although it was morning now and the streets crowded with people.

They found Peter and John first, and the two of them ran back to the garden, John in the lead because he was younger and faster. They, too, ventured inside the empty tomb and saw the burial sheets piled up in a corner of the cave.

After they had left in amazement, Mary Magdalene stayed behind, weeping, for she still did not know what to believe. After all, she had seen Jesus die on the cross with her own eyes. How could she accept what the angel had told her?

Suddenly she heard a noise behind her and, turning round, saw a man standing by the entrance to the tomb.

He said, 'Lady, why are you weeping? Who are you looking for?'

Thinking he was the gardener, she sobbed, 'If you have carried my Lord away, please tell me where you have laid him.'

The man said, 'Mary.'

And, all at once, Mary Magdalene realised

it was Jesus himself standing there in front of her.

'Master!' she cried joyfully.

When Jesus left her she ran again all the way to the disciples. But this time she burst in on them, crying out, 'I have seen our Lord!'

CHAPTER TWENTY-THREE

Jesus appears to his followers,
then leaves this world forever

Later, on the same day, two of the disciples were
walking to a village called Emmaus, which
was about seven miles west of Jerusalem so the
setting sun was in their eyes as they went. They
were discussing the extraordinary events of the
day when a stranger joined them. At least, they
thought he was a stranger.

He asked them, 'What is it you were talking
about?

They stopped and stood still, faces tight with
misery. One of them, called Cleopas, exclaimed,
'You must be the only visitor to Jerusalem who
doesn't know what's been happening over the last
few days!'

'What has been happening?' asked the stranger.

They told him the whole story of Jesus of
Nazareth and how they had hoped he would be
their Saviour but that three days ago he had been
crucified. This morning, though, some women had

gone to the tomb and found the body gone and one had seen a vision of an angel who had told her he was alive. Now they hardly knew what to believe.

At this, the stranger began to talk to them about Jesus and how all that they had described had been foretold by the prophets. They walked along together as the stranger talked, and eventually they arrived at Emmaus. The stranger was about to go on when the two disciples invited him into the house to eat supper with them.

The stranger came inside and sat at the table with them. He took up a piece of bread and, as they watched, he blessed the bread, broke it and offered it to them.

All at once they saw it was Jesus who had been walking with them and was now sitting beside them. But, in that moment of realisation, he vanished. They reminded each other how their hearts had lifted in his company, and, jumping up there and then, they raced all the way back to Jerusalem to tell the good news to the other disciples.

They found eleven of them gathered together in a locked room because they were still afraid of being arrested. Cleopas and his friend had just begun to describe what had happened to them when Jesus himself was once more standing among them.

'Peace be with you,' he said. But they thought they were seeing a ghost and were terrified.

So then he scolded them for their lack of belief and told them to touch him. 'A ghost doesn't have flesh and blood as I do.' He showed them where the nails had been in his wrists and his feet, and his side where the spear had pierced.

Still the disciples thought it too good to be true, so Jesus asked them for something to eat and, before their eyes, he ate some grilled fish. Then they knew he couldn't be a ghost.

Before he left, he prayed, 'Let the Holy Spirit come upon you and if you forgive any man's sins they shall be forgiven.'

One of the disciples, Thomas from Cana, was not with the rest of them that evening. He was extremely doubtful that Jesus had appeared. 'Until I can put my fingers where the nails were and where the spear pierced,' he said, 'I will not believe you.'

Eight more days went by and the disciples were once more gathered behind locked doors when Jesus appeared again. 'Peace be with you,' he said, as he had before. And then he turned to Thomas. 'Reach out and put your fingers in my hands and in my side.'

Thomas did so and, filled with faith, cried out, 'My Lord and my God!'

Jesus said, 'You believe because you can see me. Blessed are those who have not seen and yet still believe.'

Not long afterwards, Peter and Thomas, John, James and Nathaniel were fishing on the Lake of Tiberias. They were out in the boat all night but caught nothing. At daybreak when a faint light was silvering the water, they saw the dark silhouette of a man standing on the shore.

He called out to them, 'Have you caught anything?'

They shouted back, 'No. Nothing!'

'Cast your net over to the right and you'll soon make a catch.'

They did this and found there were so many fish in the net they could not drag it on board.

Then John recognised the stranger. 'It is the Lord!' he told Peter, and Peter was so excited that he jumped into the water to get there quicker for they were about a hundred metres out. The rest of them followed in the boat, dragging the net behind them.

When they were ashore, they found a fire already lit. Jesus told them to bring some of the fish they had caught and have breakfast with him. Peter hauled up the net over the side of the boat and, although he counted hundred and fifty-three big fish, it did not break. This miracle made all the disciples understand it was their Lord who had come to them once more.

After they had finished eating, Jesus asked Peter three times whether he loved him, as if he didn't believe Peter's word, and each time Peter became more anxious until he cried, 'You know everything! You know that I love you!' Now Peter had made up for the three times he had denied that he knew Jesus.

After Jesus' resurrection, he reappeared to his disciples over a period of forty days, which was the same length of time he had spent fasting in the wilderness before he started teaching.

On one occasion he came to them on the top of a high mountain in Galilee. He told them, 'I have been given power over heaven and earth. Therefore I tell you to go out and teach all nations, baptising the people in the name of the Father, the Son and the Holy Spirit. Teach them to love and serve God, which means they should behave as I have taught you. And remember, I am with you, always, even until the end of the world.'

Jesus' last appearance took place in the little hill-top village of Bethany where he had so often stayed with Martha and Mary. Knowing he was leaving our world for ever this time, he told his disciples to return to Jerusalem to gather their strength and wait for the Holy Spirit, who would soon come to them bringing them new courage. 'You shall be my witnesses,' he said, 'in Jerusalem and all over the world.'

Then, stretching out his hands, he blessed them and as he did so, he rose up into the sky and a cloud came between him and his disciples. They continued to gaze upwards for a long time until at length, certain that he had really gone, they started the walk back to Jerusalem.

The man called Jesus was seen no more on earth. His life here had ended. But the Holy Spirit came to his disciples, as he had promised them, and they were filled with faith and strength.

Now they felt brave enough to go out and teach the message of hope and everlasting life that Jesus had taught them.

In this way, Jesus' story has never finished but continues even to this day.

MAP OF ANCII